Walk to the

Mark Randall

Matthew Randall

ISBN-13:978-1518834714

ISBN-10:151883471X

To Craig,

one step at a time,

for every step you take is worth a thousand of mine.

Acknowledgements

The idea for writing a book came about through the amazing encouragement I received from many friends on Facebook. To you all I am hugely grateful.

My Walk to the Rock would not have been possible without the support of the Commanding Officer and All Ranks of the Royal Gibraltar Regiment. My most sincere thanks for fully participating in my venture.

To Major (Retired) Freddie Pitto, the Regimental Secretary, I am eternally grateful for securing funding for my project from the Gibunco Group – 50 years of giving back to the community! Your generosity made my walk and this book possible.

To Michelle, my wife, for encouraging me to follow my true path – I am eternally yours.

Mark

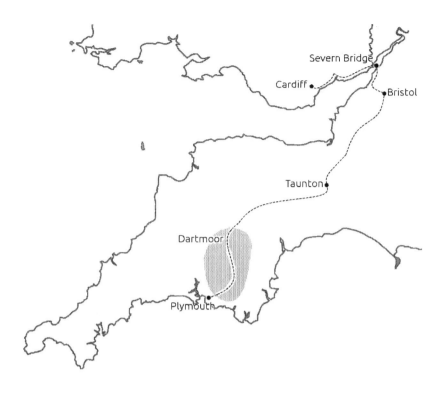

UK Route Map

Spain Route Map

Cardiff to Gibraltar
Charity Walk
2015

Oh where ha'e ye been, Lord Randall my son?

O where ha'e ye been, my handsome young man?

I ha'e been to the wild wood: mother, make my bed soon,

For I'm weary wi' hunting, and fain wald lie down.

~Anonymous, Lord Randall~

Contents

Introduction

As a teenager I read The Canterbury Tales and was taken by the idea of being on the road with fellow pilgrims, sharing a common purpose and destination. At the time of my first Camino I was filled with doubts, with who I was, with all the thousand things I was used to doing. Would I find anything worthwhile on the road? Was I wasting my time, giving up a well paid job with regular hours to plod along a well worn track? What did I want out of this Camino to Santiago?

I think that for a long time it is this purpose, this deeper understanding which has eluded me. My Walk to the Rock had a purpose, a focus to attain not just my goal, but perhaps something more – something that even now I can't quite put into words.

Travelling through the Camino I connected with other pilgrims facing troubles far worse than my own. My problems shrunk into insignificance. I realized time and again how fortunate I was.

This book proposes two tales; My diary of events and another account, something I whiled away the hours concocting while walking. That is, the story of Sandals-Grey and the Ark of Cardiff. A mind-boggling yarn full of acts of heroism, of astonishing deeds, and a great strength of feet.

I hope you enjoy reading about my Walk to the Rock as much as I enjoyed walking it!

Walk to the Rock

1

Prologue

"It is good to have an end to journey toward; but it is the
journey that matters, in the end."

~Ursula K. LeGuin, To the Ice~

September 2009, Camino Francés. Tobias finished his drink
and said "everything changes and stays the same, we have to
learn how to overcome the obstacles we find on the way."

For days I meditated over his words, unable to understand
how so shaken and afflicted by immense personal tragedy he
could find it in him to embark on this journey.

Starting from his home town in Austria, and despite having
no clear destination or notion of what he truly searched for,
he would continue walking.

Tobias told me how his wife and two young children had
been killed in a traffic accident. He was searching for
answers to questions that no man should have to find an
answer for. He said he regretted driving that day, he
regretted taking the route he took, regretted scolding his
children, not telling his wife how much he really loved her.

I did not appreciate the impact Tobias' words would have
upon me. What changes, what obstacles had he referred to?
If anything, perhaps, I understood then how unprepared I
was for what lay ahead.

I had 30% physical disability rising from numerous back
ailments due to injuries sustained throughout my military
career. The doctors said it would only get worse. Uncertain of
my future, reluctant to part with my uniform, I finally

accepted a medical discharge and retired after twenty-six years in the army.

The military door closed for me.

For years I had thought about walking the Camino. Packing a few things into a small rucksack we made our way to Roncesvalles in the Spanish Pyrenees. My son Matthew and I embarked on my first of many pilgrimages to Santiago de Compostela, the Way of Saint James.

At Headley Court, the Defence Medical Rehabilitation Centre, I was taught how to exercise to prevent further injury. I had to avoid impact on my back, contact sports, anything that might shock or jolt my spine. Walking was one of the things they deemed good.

In 2009 I walked the Camino de Santiago, a journey of some thirty-three days. In Pamplona my son developed a nasty infection from badly blistered feet and abandoned the walk.

After I parted company with Matt I suffered from painful blisters, spasms in my back, and an abscess on my groin that necessitated medical intervention. For four days I rested in the town of Sahagún, my backside jabbed full of painkillers, sleeping on the ground and pissing in a bottle.

I had to rely on the kindness of strangers to bring my meals and aid me from the floor. The doctor advised that I should abandon all hope of completing my pilgrimage, and should return home.

If I did not overcome these difficulties I knew I would most likely never return. On the fourth day I hobbled out onto the trail.

This first Camino was my hardest.

On the advice of a Swiss pilgrim on his seventh Camino I purchased a pair of walking sandals. What a difference! Over the next days my feet healed, my walking improved, and ever since my foot wear of choice has been the humble sandal.

Planning for Walk to the Rock began early in January 2015. I scribbled more than a few inklings on the back of an envelope. There was much to do and little time till the gun salute. I wanted to raise funds for the Royal Gibraltar Regiment Benevolent Fund, and a second charity – the Gibraltar Broadcasting Corporation Open Day. The ideal start point for my walk, Cardiff – the gun salute would set me off with a bang!

At the top of my list of notes was – form a committee! Our first meeting was basically agreeing on who would be doing what. The Commanding Officer, Lieutenant Colonel Ivor Lopez agreed to talk to the press and brought on board his Adjutant, Captain John Pitto. Francis Brancato would draft a letter for all potential sponsors, I would be left to focus on the walk.

Training started that very January, 20-25 kilometres three times a week with increasing weight. I discarded anything considered a luxury, packing and repacking to obtain the right balance of weight versus self-sufficiency. This walk would be unsupported, meaning I would carry all my kit, all my lifelines on my back.

Walking for many days on end is certainly not for everyone. I have heard many a pilgrim say "this is my first and last Camino". The long road to Santiago is a roller coaster of physical hardship and emotional suffering ending the dreams of many. The Way of Saint James can be a very rewarding experience or a punishing trial.

Including Walk to the Rock, I have now walked 7500 km just on the Caminos, my daughter Tammy joining me for some 2500 of those. The Caminos provided a conduit for my energy and pent up frustrations in life, so I kept on returning, looking for more.

People are understandably curious, often asking why pilgrims chose to go on such a journey. The answer is not simple, nor is it complex. The Camino is a religious and a spiritual pilgrimage where many find solace, find hope for their future. They find the path in life that they want to walk.

Santiago is the goal for hundreds of thousands of pilgrims. The remains of Saint James have been laid up in the great cathedral of the holy city for more than a thousand years. Those who would pay homage need only reach out for that field under the stars!

During my 2015 Cardiff to Gibraltar Charity Walk I jotted down descriptions of the route, of people, and of conversations that struck me in any particular way. As I flicked through the pages of the notebook I realised there were a hundred more stories waiting to be told!

2

Cardiff to Plymouth

"When in April the sweet showers fall...
Then people long to go on pilgrimages."
~Chaucer, The Canterbury Tales~

Day 1: Cardiff to Newport – 27 km

Walked through the centre of Cardiff towards the castle wearing a new pair of sandals – the gun salute was at midday. Before leaving the hotel I'd checked under the bed, in the wardrobe, and bathroom. Everything I would carry for the next 75 days was now in my backpack. Far too heavy. Should I ditch my jacket? Could I toss a pair of socks or two? Couldn't get rid of anything in my medkit, that much was certain.

My toes wriggled, I put a foot up on one of the benches and tightened a strap on my very light North Face sandals, bought just yesterday at an outdoor specialist down the street. At the castle a dozen or so men formed a half circle, as I approached they called out to me by name. Captain John Pitto busily briefed the group of veterans on the day's events – joined them, anxious and waiting for the starting gun.

We entered the forecourt together, I went to the information desk asking if they had a stamp for my credentials. "A stamp?" The young man behind the counter gave me an odd look. "We don't do stamps, you'll have to go to the post office for that." I offered further explanation – this was not an ordinary stamp, well, it was – just not that sort. The credentials I wanted stamped are also known as the credencial del peregrino, the pilgrim credential or passport, a booklet containing the stamped start point for the pilgrimage to Santiago de Compostela. These credentials ought to be stamped once a day and twice over the last hundred kilometres. The many albergues,* bars, or churches along the Camino are more than willing to produce their own unique stamp for any pilgrim that asks. At the Pilgrim Office in Santiago de Compostela the credencial is validated and la Compostela presented – a certificate awarded by the Church for completing a pilgrimage.

The young chap rifled through drawers under the counter, eventually producing a small rectangular piece of rubber, presumably once attached to a traditional wooden stamp. He pressed it against a dry ink pad and onto my credentials smudging a badly faded impression of Cardiff Castle and the barely visible words 'Cardiff' beneath. Good enough.

Tammy arrived by taxi wearing her new dress (one I was forced to buy the previous day, along with new shoes, new handbag, and a new skirt just in case the dress wouldn't do), she looked stunning – very grown up. Oh dear, time most certainly flies. Looking at her I felt old, maybe too old, too worn out to be doing this 2200 kilometre trek! Grey in my beard, I'd had to roll myself out of bed and use a chair to help get the bag on my back.

For the pre-gun salute reception we were escorted to the museum below the castle cafeteria area. Chatted to the Lord Mayor of Cardiff, the Lord Lieutenant, to Deputy Mayor Kaiane Aldorino Gibraltar's very own Miss World 2009, and Samantha Sacramento, a Gibraltar government minister.

The clock in the castle grounds struck midday. The first gun fired in salute, a resounding thunderous honour to the birthday of Her Majesty the Queen. The turnout and drill of

*Hostel for pilgrims.

the gun teams under command of Major Ian Martinez, Firing Point Officer, was absolutely top notch. Twenty-one guns sounded in salvo.

Said my farewell to Colonel Ivor, gave Tammy a big hug and kiss on the cheek. How I hate farewells. After so many years of departing for long periods on tours of duty I was no nearer to being able to snap back those sharp emotions which tight squeeze my chest when I know those I love are not at hand. Down the main street, down past the hotel, down towards the Severn, I felt a rising thirst for the walk.

The first 6 km exiting Cardiff were difficult. Crossed motorways moving mainly through heavily built-up areas looking for signs of the Wales Coast Path. Weather perfect, sun shining and a light breeze made for ideal walking conditions. The route I had chosen led me towards the Severn Estuary, in the distance – England. Out of the city, into the wilderness of run-down trailer parks complete with burnt out husks of cars and rusted soda cans. Walked on a path on the side of a road for a time, the trail slowly improved – got to Newport, my stop for the first night. Nice bit of cod for supper – love my fish, every chance I'd get along this route I would ask for fish of some description. Everything ached – my knees and thighs were tense, every part stiff from the first days exertions. My head hurt, I was worried and it showed – a good night's rest and I'd be raring to go!

Did not sleep well that night, rolling around in bed thinking of the year before. In 2014 I embarked from Canterbury with the intention of making it all the way to Rome. Had not made it. Fears were eating away inside me.

The route ahead would not be direct to Gibraltar – I'd made it my goal to walk via Santiago de Compostela. Might as well collect stamps for my pilgrim passport along the way.

Looking at the first page with Cardiff Castle smeared inexpertly a certain sense of trepidation arose.

Stamp Number One – not a good start!

Cardiff Castle – start gun

Day 2: Newport to M48 Service Station – 40 km

There was an alternative bridge-crossing a few kilometres up ahead but I wanted a ride on the transporter bridge over the River Usk. In 2013 I had hitched a ride on another of its kind in Bilbao whilst walking the Camino del Norte.

Got my ticket, boarded the gondola as the only foot passenger, and, after they loaded a single car we were off – the first crossing of the day. Glanced back and was presented with a magnificent view of the transporter bridge; enormous pylons with a length of steel suspended high above the waters.

Keeping a riverside course for a good chunk of the morning I headed inland at a relaxed pace, eventually reaching the Severn Estuary coastline. Lucky it was a clear day, could make out buildings on the English side across the river. A refreshing breeze at my back helped me along the path. Stopped and watched sea birds feeding on the mud flats.

Far ahead, the M4 motorway bridge connecting England to Wales. This was not my crossing point, the M48 Severn Bridge another 5 km beyond. There was only the path ahead, simple enough. Diversion – a sign notified walkers the coastal trail was closed due to works. Had to leave the path and head inland in the wrong direction. A few kilometres later the signs led me across the motorway, then in another direction, and back across the same motorway to the coastal trail. Took about an hour and a half. The bridge seemed pretty far away.

Tammy called to say that Johann, my nephew, had been involved in a nasty traffic accident in Gibraltar. Day 2 and I felt my spirits dwindle, had hit a low point so early in the walk. The news of the accident, the extra unplanned distance, sore feet from new sandals all were taking a toll.

Was not where I wanted to be, but pressed on. The path led to a field with a sign that said 'Private – No Trespassing'. Ignored the warning and cut through to the edge of a hill, hauled my rucksack to the other side of the barbed wire fence and jumped.

Heard voices, three youths gave me puzzled glances, one fed firewood to the glowing embers of a makeshift bonfire. They stood glued to the spot and stared. Greeted them, made a joke about the fire and asked for directions. Ahead, the motorway suspension bridge.

Crossed in the dark. Felt the cold. Stopped, put my warm jacket on. Rain, stopped again and swapped jackets. A wind blew high on the walkway. Crosses tied to the railings marked where people had jumped into the Severn Estuary.

Arrived at the Travelodge, wet, tired, having walked more than I'd planned. Three blisters on my left foot, one on my right. So much for my new sandals!

Turned and shifted checking my watch every half hour. The night stretched on. Struggled with visions of failure, of slipping and cracking a foot. It had happened before, it could happen again tomorrow. I lay for long minutes and hours dreary eyed staring at the ceiling.

Day 3: M48 Service Station to Winford – 35 km

Got out of bed, felt the pain – my feet hurt. The sharp sting from the blisters was already almost unbearable.

Walked the coastal path on the English side; the Severn Way, heading for Bristol. Terrain varied from rocks and gravel to hard tarmac making it tough going on my sore feet.

The River Avon and over the Clifton Suspension Bridge. Had been here years earlier, attending a short course at Bristol University on European Security and Terrorism.

My feet were burning, took my shoes off and slapped on some Vaseline. The new sandals were condemned to the bottom of my bag, now wore a pair of lightweight walking shoes – tried and tested. Had left my old sandals with Tammy. Kept repeating, "It will be better tomorrow, endure".

Day 4: Winford to Stoughton Cross – 30 km

Followed country lanes, past a few farms and through cultivated land. At the bottom of a hill the ground opened up and extended to a steep rock face. The path ended at a small car park where I saw several families with dogs preparing to trek along the Cheddar Gorge.

Seeing the dogs reminded me of Poppy, the most loyal four-legged companion anyone could have wished for. She was a mixed breed, part Spanish Water Dog. Years ago Poppy and I hiked across the Llanos de Líbar, a trail sandwiched between a range of peaks running from Montejaque to Cortes de la Frontera in Andalucía. Mich dropped us off and the plan was she'd later pick us up at Cortes. It was summer, started early but the sun soon became unbearable.

More than a few kilometres on, I noticed Poppy stopping in every scrap of shade. She finally lay down, refused to move at all, with that sad look in her eyes that only dogs seem to have. After a short tug-o-war she reluctantly got to her paws and followed on, only to lay down at the next shaded area. The hot road had burnt her paws, fat bulging blisters must have made it extraordinarily painful to take even a single step. Patched her up and did the only thing I could – slung her across my shoulders and walked on.

A well fed mid-size dog of 15 to 20 kilos! The day got hotter, the path ascended forcing frequent stops. No more water. The only way out for my four-legged companion was on my two legs, Poppy scratched for both of us. During one of her rampant knee jerking episodes I unwittingly took the wrong path. Something was not quite right, the sun was in the wrong place.

Resting by a rusty fence we were alerted by alarming growls, fast approaching in close formation were countless cerdos ibéricos! I ran, heard a yelp and stopped – never leave a fallen comrade behind!

Poppy limped after me, the pigs pushed on the fence, growling and snorting up a storm. Was like the scene from Hannibal with the man-eating pigs. Shouldered the poor mutt once more and we hobbled off as one.

Lost, my injured pooch on my shoulders, no food, no water, worried what Mich would think when we did not turn up. I called, no reply. Was her mobile charged? Or, more likely, lost at the bottom of her bag?

Further on, much further, I spied a woman laying out food on a table in the middle of a cork forest. Corcheros were at work in the vicinity collecting cork, and she was preparing their meal. With a few kind words we were watered, fed, and pointed towards the proper road. Cars sped by, I thumbed for a lift. It was hours past meet-up time. Exhausted, I dragged Poppy on her lead with great effort.

A young man, son of a wealthy landowner, pulled up in his 4×4 and took us the 10 km to Cortes de la Frontera. We were four hours late. From this experience I deduced that Poppy must go on a diet, that Michelle needed a smaller handbag, and that I might need a compass the next time I took the dog for a walk!

Cheddar Gorge – the road twisted and turned through the steep hills and high cliffs. Watched some goats scramble up the rock face with ease and felt envious of their agility. I have often jumped from rock to rock whilst out hiking ignoring the dangers of falling or twisting an ankle. Took a moment, a picture, and thanked Cheddar for its cheese.

At Nut Tree Farm, Anne brought some fresh milk and I made a lovely cup of tea. The room was in a quaint old farmhouse in tranquil countryside.

Sat with Melvyn, my host and a Master Wood Turner, in a very cosy living room. Spoke for a long time about my walk, his work, spirituality, and how to find balance in life. Melvyn warned of the resident ghost; after all, it was a 16th century farmhouse! Took a bath and went to bed. The ghost never came. Most likely scared off by my snoring went in search of one of the students attending Melvyn's wood-turning course.

Felt I was finding my rhythm, blisters healing after more stabs than a picador* to a bull. The first few days are usually the hardest. It wasn't the nature of the ground or the distance, just getting used to walking day after day with weight on your back, finding a rhythm and being at ease with the adventure. I knew this was crunch time, I had to overcome my fears and pain, endure!

*Someone who antagonizes a bull in the bullring, stabbing it with a lance from horseback.

26

Day 5: Stoughton Cross to Bridgwater – 30 km

Unable to connect to the internet I had not posted my reports for a few days. It was encouraging to see such overwhelming support from so many people on Facebook.

Went over green rolling countryside and ploughed fields. Arrived at the edge of Bridgwater, a man pasting election posters confirmed the correct direction. This is something I do very regularly in towns and cities, even if certain of my way I prefer to confer with locals. I have discovered many alternative routes and interesting places to visit – information I could not have found from guidebooks or online.

Today was blessed with glorious weather and a refreshing light rain. My feet were better and a smile returned to my face.

Day 6: Bridgwater to Wellington – 30 km

I shift and turn searching for a comfortable position but sleep does not come. A golf ball alleviates the chronic pain on my neck. Between my knees a pillow, a 3-pronged massage contraption hard pressed against the small of my back. At home only aggressive massages at the hands of Matt are able to give me some small respite.

I move, the golf ball thunks onto the floor. Have to switch the lights on to look for it. Watch reads 0230 hrs. 0450 hrs, still turning and shifting. Can't wait for dawn, for light and getting back on the trail.

Stuck with minor roads and though they were longer it was considerably faster. The terrain was flat, the meat grinder effect of ploughed fields a distant memory. My phone rang, Michelle. Told her of my night – she laughs and says "well, at least I didn't have to put up with it". It rained, put on my waterproofs.

There is something special about walking in the rain which I have always enjoyed. The hood over my head a cocoon limiting visibility. All I could hear were rain drops lightly falling all around and my shoes on the tarmac. Walked the northern periphery of Taunton, stayed clear of the centre to try and make good time on the road.

Back in May of 2013 I was walking the Camino del Norte and it rained for 25 out of 30 days. Clothes permanently damp, feet soaked from wearing sandals, blinkered with my rain hood, almost blind from absence of glasses. In the rain, unable to focus on the Camino, I begun to look within.

Day 7: Wellington to Tiverton – 30 km

Made a pot of porridge and prepared for the day ahead. For most of the day I walked the Grand Western Canal. Navigation was easy, set myself on automatic pilot and followed the canal all the way into town. What wonderful scenery, quiet and peaceful, all I could hear were the birds and the noises that trees make.

The Grand Western Canal connects Taunton with Tiverton, cutting right through the village of Sampford Peverell. As I passed I saw a pub to my left and (with enormous willpower) withheld from stopping for a pint.

There were numerous well kept canal boats tied to moorings. I saw a memorial commemorating an air crash. Two RAF servicemen had lost their lives in 1961 near here when their Canberra came down in the canal. The pilot avoided hitting the town and thus prevented a disaster.

Made it to Tiverton in good time and rushed to the bus station. Called Tammy who got very excited – we arranged to meet at her flat in Exeter. We ate, I grabbed my trusty old sandals and rushed to catch the late bus back to Tiverton. It must have been the wine, as I dozed off on the bus remembering only the arrival at the other end. Went to bed exhausted. Pouring down outside.

Day 8: Tiverton to Yeoford – 34 km

O630 hrs. From Tiverton I followed the Exe River Valley south, down to Bickleigh. A beautiful place, lined with cottages with thatched roofs, a medieval bridge, and smart watering holes. A bit further on was Bickleigh Castle, a fortified manor house on the banks of the River Exe.

Stopped outside the arched entrance of the courtyard and tended to my feet. As the rain increased I changed into my waterproofs. Ivor Lopez called and I walked and talked and took a wrong turning, ended up stuck in mud! I scolded Ivor over the phone for getting me side-tracked. Lesson of the day; don't walk and talk on the phone!

The road followed the river and snaked up a long hill. The rain ceased, views from the top were stunning, a clear and defined vision which follows heavy rain. I had often seen similar splendour atop the Rock looking out across the Bay of Gibraltar towards Morocco, able to pinpoint houses with vivid clarity.

Here I walked through fat rolling hills crowned by scattering clouds, glistening woods descending to the river valley. Could see movement on the road connecting the dots between church tower and spire and disappearing into the distance. Spent the night at Yeoford, another great English rural village.

I was greeted by the very cheerful Winnie, proprietress of Warren's Farm. Small miracles do happen, I thought, as she offered me a pot of tea with scones, clotted cream, and jam. Wow! Thinking all day how much I wanted a good cuppa. Was she a mind reader or was it just tea time? Winnie's home-made dinner was superb, her breakfast exceptional. By the photograph of father and son hanging in the dining room I deduced her son had recently been commissioned from Sandhurst. Coincidence? Most certainly!

Day 9: Yeoford to Chagford – 24 km

Poured incessantly until mid afternoon. A good set of waterproofs and a hearty breakfast went a long way in keeping me going.

Drewsteignton, a mid-morning snack (well and a bit more) – brew, packet of crisps, a muffin, and the most scrumptious Cornish pasty ever! Sat on a bench outside the little post office shop and was joined by the village cat – it crawled onto my lap, climbed up the table and took an interest in my pasty and muffin. Shoved it away, it meowed and dug into my rucksack. In the end we shared the muffin, bits of Cornish pasty, and it licked clean the empty crisp wrapper. Had to fight the feline fiend for my last bit of tea!

Up a steep hill, across a field, through woods, found myself slack jawed at the stunning sight of the Teign Gorge. The path was not easy to follow. Ended up walking all the way to Castle Drogo by accident. Later found that Castle Drogo was the last ever castle to be built in England, finished a scant hundred years ago.

Unsure of precisely where I should be heading, the official from the National Trust Office graciously gave directions out of the castle grounds and back onto the track. I mean, I knew precisely where I was, and where I wanted to be, just, well the bits in between might be a little fuzzy.

Descended and crossed a group of day ramblers, they confirmed my heading and, a bit further on along the trail I marvelled at a sign that read – GIB HOUSE – was this a coincidence? No! There was a higher power at work here, sending little signs and making sure I did not stray too far from the path! Well, alright, maybe a little bit of a coincidence, a little bit of a divine intervention.

Got to my destination for the day – just in time for a late lunch. Adie O'Shea had called, said he would like to join me for a couple of days on the trail. He dressed for the occasion, pack and walking boots. Alas, he'd not forgotten his phone, and work commitments would not allow him to stay. Hmm, had he cunningly planned his escape? Most likely! Harked back to when, in Canada in November 1993, Adrian formed part of my team ascending Mount Athabasca in the Colombia Icefield of Jasper National Park. A hard slog through deep snow, I called the team to a halt and went over a ridge to scout ahead. On returning I found Adie puffing merrily away polluting the natural habitat.

"Well, I've brought them all the way up so might as well smoke, sir." That was his excuse. Well Adie, you're all dressed up in Chagford, so following your logic, might as well walk! He always had a way out of a sticky situation, very sharp bloke.

Adie walked with me from the car park to the pub where we exercised extensively by lifting a pint glass to our lips. I didn't want to be blamed for his dehydration from the effort! Had a good lunch of pork belly with apple sauce, reminisced about our regimental days and shared a great few hours together. Ridiculous as it sounds, this was the day I had my first beer!

Day 10: Chagford to Scorriton – 33 km

The route wound through minor roads and the Two Moors Way. Snaking through valleys, over meandering rivers, up the tors through quaint hamlets. The Two Moors Way is a long distance route between Ivybridge, on the southern edge of Dartmoor, and Lynmouth, on the north coast of Exmoor. Dartmoor is an area of exceptional unspoilt beauty, of wondrous wildlife, and long stretches of welcome solitude and tranquillity.

Sat on a grassy knoll, took my sandals off and was having a snack when a group of walkers approached. Said hello to the two lead ladies, one of them gave me a funny look and asked "are you Gibraltarian?"

I was in awe, how did she know? Another mind reader? Eureka! It dawned on me; it takes one to know one! I replied "yes, you too?"

This group of six ramblers were training for a trek in Minorca. Rosemarie Ferrary-Davis told me she was from Gibraltar. She turned to the others and said "I told you, there are Gibraltarians everywhere!"

What are the chances of meeting another llanito[*] in the middle of Dartmoor eh? Quite good apparently, another sign! They all were very supportive, digging into their pockets and donating.

Of course I took a picture – Chris Davis, Heather Taylor, Col Bill McDermott RM,[+] no shoes – will travel (me!), Rosemarie, Katherine McDermott-Darley, and Dr Graham Taylor.

---

*People from the Rock. Also, Llanito is a form of spoken Gibraltarian, a mixture of English/Spanish and Genoese.
+Royal Marines.

Friends of Gibraltar in Dartmoor

Stayed at the Tradesman's Arms in Scorriton. Another chance encounter – Richard Copus, staunch supporter of Gibraltar and acquaintance of Dr Garcia, the Deputy Chief Minister. He kindly organised an interview with the Western Morning News, which I had over the phone with Kate Langston. Malcolm, the barman at the Tradesman's Arms, gave me a fiver for charity, and Mark, the manager refused to charge for my food. We formed a team for the weekly pub quiz; Richard, Malcolm, and myself, and came very close to answering some questions correctly.

Day 11: Scorriton to Ivybridge – 24 km

Set off before first light. Cold, wet, and horribly windy. Rain hard against my face, visibility very poor and this was quite problematic as I could not find north with my watch (by using the hour and minute hand).

Lugged my water logged rucksack up a steep section of the path. The ground was soft and wet, sheep lying and feeding all around enjoying the slippery grass much more than I was!

This was hill walking in its purest sense, the kind of walking I enjoy the most.

The inevitable. Two hours from where I'd started, and after a long hill climb, I could not find the path. Took a hamlet moment (for those of you who are old enough to remember the advert), without the cigar and sat by some rocks at the very top of a tor trying to take refuge from the wind and rain. Could see no sky, looked at my map and moved it around and around. Saw evidence of a stream flowing perpendicular to the high ground, could I use this to find my way? Clearly one of the many occasions I wish I'd not discarded my compass from the packing list!

A shape, a human silhouette, what luck! From yonder an angel sent to deliver me from the wilderness. Katie was walking and practising her navigation skills with her silver compass. She was pretty sure where we were, from there I managed to set a new course. My assumptions on the stream below had also been correct (of course!).

Halted for the day at Ivybridge, a town on the southern edge of Dartmoor. Settled into my accommodation in a pub and went looking for the tourist information to get maps of the area.

Passing the entrance of a supermarket I noticed a young man sat on the ground sopping wet. By his side a little dog and a large rucksack, shoppers walked by oblivious to his presence. Janko was from Slovakia, roaming around the country looking for employment, for a new life. He hadn't eaten for two days, but was not begging or asking anyone for anything.

I asked what he wanted to eat, but he was not particular. Bought him some food and drink and handed over a tenner. Janko asked why I was being so kind to him – replied because I could. Because if I ever found myself in a similar situation I hoped others would do the same.

Yesterday I mentioned that at the Tradesman's Arms in Scorriton the owner and barman were very generous towards my cause. On the way I have met many others who have been equally kind and charitable. Thank you, Anne/Melvyn from Nut Tree Farm, Stoughton Cross, what a breakfast! Thank you Winnie from Warrens Farm, Yeoford, thanks for the scrumptious supper. Many thanks to Fran from Ring O'Bells, Chagford, and Rosemarie Ferrary-Davis and friends. You have all made my walk through the South West so much brighter than the weather permitted!

Tomorrow, Plymouth.

Day 12: Ivybridge to Plymouth – 25 km

Was met by my daughter Tammy and her friends Roberta Keane, Richard King, and Jake Howells. Richard navigated and I relaxed, talking for most of the way. We followed country lanes, getting to Plymouth in time for a good pub lunch.

Plymouth had been one of the embarkation points for English pilgrims going to Santiago for many hundreds of years. I shall be embarking tomorrow, part of history, right? More or less. I took photographs of the large scallop shell depicting the pilgrimage to Santiago de Compostela, the pier where the Mayflower had set sail, and the green on Plymouth Hoe where Raleigh bowled when he received news of the invincible Spanish Armada, not!

Tammy, Jake, Richard, and Roberta – Plymouth

Day 13: Plymouth to Santander

Tammy stayed for the night, we went out for a few drinks and the next morning said farewell. At the Ferry port I boarded, got to my cabin, and went exploring the M/V Pont Aven.

Going towards Santander to meet an old friend, couldn't help but remember brothers-in-law Juan and Jose from Gran Canaria, whom I'd parted company with in that very city. Met them in 2013 at the start of the Camino del Norte in Irún. Both retired, Jose was in the petroleum industry and Juan was ashamed to admit he had been a banker, disgusted with the recent cases of corruption involving Spanish banks.

Jose almost abandoned the walk. On my advice they took a bus to Oviedo and engaged on the Camino Primitivo. Every night they called and said how much they were enjoying the new trail. We remain in touch to this day.

3
Camino del Norte

"No one saves us but ourselves. No one can and no one may.
We ourselves must walk the path."

~Buddha~

During May/June 2013 I walked some 860 kilometres of
the Camino del Norte from Irún (bordering France), to
Santiago de Compostela. The Camino del Norte follows la
costa Cantábrica, hugging the shore line from coastal town to
town. It is a beautiful Camino passing through many
wonderful cities; San Sebastian, Bilbao, Guernika,
Santander, and Gijón.

The Camino eventually leaves the coast and winds south-
west through the interior of Galicia. An isolated area where
pilgrims can easily get lost on the remote forest routes. The
best albergue I have ever visited is to be found here, just
before Santander at a place called Güemes. Padre Ernesto
and his team of volunteers made me feel very welcome and
right at home at la Cabaña del Abuelo Peuto.

I ended that Camino with my good friend Helmut who hailed
from South Tirol. He had a thick German accent and
Austrian ancestry. Many in the Tirol region never really felt
Italian, wished for independence or re-unification with
Austria. Helmut and I spend a week walking, entering
Santiago together.

Day 14: Santander to Mompia – 10 km

After a 24 hour ferry ride I disembarked at Santander. Rough seas had made my sea voyage unpleasant, feeling a little dizzy, glad to be back on solid ground. An old boss and a good mate was waiting– Francis Brancato. Keen to get on the trail we set off, late as it was, pushed on about 10 km to Mompia. Moved through the urban melee of Santander, putting ourselves in a good position for the next day.

Back in January when I first mentioned the walk Francis did not hesitate, said he would support the venture and join me at the first opportunity. Here he was, true to his word.

Twelve days in the UK had taken its toll. The ferry crossing gave me time to think, about the walk so far, about the journey ahead. The end still so far away.

Knew I would have to guard myself against the false cresting syndrome (a feeling of premature accomplishment), and the complacency which followed. Completing the UK phase was a big step, just that. On this rugged coast all I held in my eyes was the journey ahead – the path stretching off into the days and weeks and months. I did not sleep well that night.

The next morning I awoke and truly appreciated having Francis with me. My mood changed for the better, I would take my Camino day by day, step by step.

Day 15: Mompia to Santillana del Mar – 28 km

There are three lies about Santillana del Mar; that it isn't santa (holy), it isn't llana (flat) and nowhere near the mar (sea)!

"Randall, you weren't still all night, writhing like a worm on a hook! What was that thud, eh?" Francis laughed, "three times I heard a bang!" I explained it was my golf ball. It had rolled off the bed, told about the difficulties I had getting to sleep with my back. He now understood why I had suggested separate rooms.

Walked at a steady pace, felt a world of difference between yesterday and today. The effects of the long sea journey and sea-sickness tablets wore off, we walked and talked. Francis really enjoyed being here, made good progress and saw few pilgrims along the way. Remembered my previous time through the area and pointed out places I had visited.

In 2013 I stopped at a camping site at the top of a long hill 1 km past town. At a bar by the main square I befriended a lovely couple who owned the place. Two policemen walked in with the Alcalde, the Mayor, and from there on my glass never emptied! Raúl, the owner, refused to let me walk back up the hill to the camp, taking me in his car. Angelina gifted a jar of home-made rosemary ointment. "It will soothe your feet after a long day's walk," she said.

Nearing the day's end Francis had a sudden craving for a glass of milk. To his pleasant surprise I took him to a little place at the entrance to town. We had a tall glass of fresh milk with a wedge of quesada – a popular pudding from Cantabria, similar to a cheesecake. A sweet end to a good day.

Day 16: Santillana del Mar to San Vicente de la Barquera – 32 km

Through lush green fields, wooded areas, picturesque rolling countryside, all within proximity of the sea. On occasions the route took us very close to the shore, crossing a beach. It wasn't until about five hours after the start that we stopped at the first place we found in Cóbreces.

Sat outside, the table next to us occupied by fellow pilgrims. There wasn't much on offer so we had a drink, some crisps, and a bocadillo de tortilla de patatas.* The barman, who we assumed was also the owner, did not have any interest whatsoever in serving the patrons. His lack of enthusiasm total. Overheard the conversation the other pilgrims were having, trying to order food, incredulous as to how indolent the waiter was. Unsatisfied with his lackadaisical attitude the pilgrims got up and left!

Passing by a narrow bridge we saw an abandoned 4-wheel drive tumbled over with an overturned trailer attached. With one voice we said – remember!? Years ago returning from the ranges in Sennybridge, Wales, our Land Rover took a nosedive into a muddy ditch, lucky that only the attached trailer overturned. Francis and I had the privilege of walking the 5 miles to the range control office where the nearest phone could be found.

Walked through a eucalyptus forest and observed the work carried out clearing large areas of trees. Made good time to Comillas, one of the best known towns in Cantabria. Passed the very impressive Capricho by Gaudi. Charged an exorbitant price for beers and snacks in the town plaza.

San Vicente de la Barquera still some kilometres away, our destination for the day, a view to behold. Approaching from the high ground we contemplated the wide ría⁺ which opened up once it passed under the long bridge leading to town. The houses and buildings ascended from sea level on the other side of the ría. Nestled at the very top of the town was a church and a castle. On the horizon – the Picos de Europa.

*Baguette-style sandwich with potato omelette.
+A drowned river valley that remains open to the sea.

Day 17: San Vicente to Llanes – 45 km

Crossed the bridge out of town, hard left, and uphill for 6 km. Ahead, the snow tipped Picos de Europa. Named so by ancient mariners, the mountain peaks were the first site of Europe for ships arriving from the Americas.

Francis, San Vicente de la Barquera – Picos de Europa

Left San Vicente de la Barquera in the knowledge that it would be a long day, kept a steady pace uphill. The route took us through small hamlets, many abandoned churches, paths, woods, and many roads.

At a bar we stopped for breakfast, sat at the barra (counter) on high chairs and ordered coffee and toast. An elderly gentlemen approached us and engaged in conversation. He was an 88 year old Austrian man accompanied by his son. They walk 200 km together every year – wow! We saw them leave carrying very light day-packs. Later as we passed another bar they were having another rest. Would I still be walking at 88?

At nearby crossroads we met a German middle aged lady sat on the ground. Her plastic water bottle had burst and we shared some of ours. She asked if she could join us for a while. Elsa had started in Santander but was finding it difficult, it had taken her more than a few days to get this far. I explained that we were walking long distances, but she insisted she would still like to walk with us.

The day got hotter, the road harder. Elsa carried a heavy pack, big camera slung round her neck, and held a weighty guide book referring to it continuously. Francis advised her to put away the book and not to worry, that I knew the way. The longest distance she had ever walked in one day was 20 km. Today she was in for a long haul, we were more than doubling that distance. I insisted she should re-think trying to keep up as we would have to slow down our pace for her benefit.

The terrain rough, the walk worthwhile. We entered a eucalyptus wood emerging on a plateau with a magnificent view of the rugged coast and a glassy sea. Followed a coastal path, traversed an exquisite post-card village and then came to an impressive spot high above a ría. Surrounded by tall pine trees we were sat overlooking an amazing body of water which weaved its way inland from the sea. I instructed Elsa to remove her boots, her feet were red and blistered. She must have been suffering but absolutely refused to quit.

Francis volunteered to carry her bag, picked it up and frowned, astonished by the weight this lady had been lugging. She never told us in detail, but Elsa made it clear that she was doing this Camino to get away. The emotional baggage she carried weighed on her far heavier than her backpack.

We assured that we would not abandon her, but soon she reached her limit, that point beyond which she could advance no further. Rested, again I insisted she take off her boots. Her feet were in a very bad state, swollen, and with weeping blisters that could lead to a nasty infection if not treated. She wore heavy mountaineering boots, the sales assistant in Germany said they were the correct footwear. I wondered whether he had ever been on the Camino! Treated her feet and we continued.

Elsa felt down in the pits, ready to call it quits. We found a place and arranged a room for her to stay, she had walked close to 40 km! Francis carried her pack for about 5 km. Bravo Francis! We advised her to get rid of some stuff, to focus on the walk, and most of all to enjoy it. By the time we got to Llanes it was 1930 hrs. We showered, fed, and went to bed knackered.

Day 18: Llanes to Ribadesella – 35 km

Woke later than usual, went for churros con chocolate.* Well rested and keen to continue, we pushed on to Ribadesella. On the rocky shoreline we saw bufones; blow-holes. Amazed by the might of the sea we stood nailed to the spot, looking as water spray gushed out on the land-ward side.

I wondered how Elsa was doing, if she'd taken our advice and was resting her feet. After the walk, some time in September Elsa got in touch with Francis and told us how she had completed her Camino. She sent us a couple of tubes of Hirschtalg, a white cream made out of deer fat used to prevent chaffed skin.

*Fritters with chocolate – a fried doughy pastry, popular throughout Spain for breakfast.

Francis and I must have gone through the complete Beatles and Eagles repertoire, then started with America and ending our impromptu concert with Simon & Garfunkel. We reminisced about our younger years, night-life in the early eighties in Gibraltar, and the red and white Starsky and Hutch car my brother Bob drove.

My best Camino singing tour ever was in 2013 while walking the French Way. Tammy and I befriended a group of Mexicans, two pairs of bothers, all cousins, led by a Columbian priest, Padre Pedro – el Jefe – who had officiated at all their weddings. They were US citizens, bilingual. They took to Tammy, taking it in turns to dance with her along the way. They lugged a solar panel to keep their boogie-box powered, could walk and sing all day, and ate like horses! They also had some of the worst blisters I had ever seen. Their faith and desire to get to Santiago kept them going. At the end of long walking days they would drink, sing, and rejoice. Once in Santiago we met up with them again and celebrated Tammy's birthday where they sang Las Mañanitas, a traditional Mexican birthday song. Best bunch of guys I have ever walked with – saludos brother peregrinos!

As Francis and I walked every field became a platoon attack waiting to happen, forming-up-place to the left, fix bayonets here, fire support over by the tree line! On the next hill we'd deployed a company defensive position on the reverse slope, trenches sighted in support of each other, machine-guns to the flanks. Oh dear! Changing our outlooks after so many years in the military is difficult, and why should we? We would have both enlisted again the next day if we could!

Day 19: Ribadesella to Villaviciosa – 36 km

My head throbbed, could it be the sidra, from last night? Packed and set off. Francis accompanied me to the edge of town where we said our farewells. Alone again.

Hills, hills, and more hills conspired to make the day's walk very challenging. The route taking me down to beaches and then up to eucalyptus forests high on coastal cliffs. Forests are abundant in the region, planted for their timber and occupying areas once covered by many other species of trees. Eucalyptus tends to dominate and eliminate the opposition.

This was a rugged coast line castigated by erosion. I wondered how many walked here and enjoyed the work of millions of years of lashing waves. Arrived at Villaviciosa after a steep and long 11 km climb, followed by a 6 km descent. It was no fun walking on this type of terrain, felt the strain on my ankles and knees going downhill and feared for the impact on my joints. Had it not been for the knee and ankle supports I could have suffered some serious damage.

Villaviciosa is well known for its cider, which Francis and I had been drinking copiously the last few days. Poured from high up to allow the amber fluid to cascade into the glass which is held well below at another arms length, sidra is drank immediately before the effervescence is lost.

Francis would by now be in Oviedo, toasting our walk with more sidra! I had another two days before I would reach Oviedo.

Day 20: Villaviciosa to Pola de Sierro – 27 km

Drastic changes in weather, terrain, and scenery. The route initially rose from the Asturian seaboard through unspoilt countryside, then over flat boring industrialized areas as I neared Oviedo.

An excessively hot day through lush countryside speckled with cattle and stone farmhouses. Generally tough, the path winds up difficult hills and descends into deep valleys. Ground was boggy from rain of previous days slowing my progress. Rewarding views from hill tops and fast flowing streams in the valleys to refresh my feet.

Took the harder option, walking the steeper slopes over the hills instead of the winding road that ran through the valley to my right. Was high up and got a birds eye view of the surrounding landscape. In the low ground stood the Monastery of Valdediós. Wondered whether it might have been easier to take the lower road, could have lodged at the monastery. Looking down I was reminded of a time during my walk on the Via Francigena in 2014, the pilgrimage from Canterbury to Rome.

On that occasion I stopped at the Benedictine Abbey of Saint Paul's in a town called Wisques, Pas-de-Calais, France. Brother Paul asked for my credentials, stamped them, and led me to a comfortable room with clean bedding and a view of the abbey grounds.

I was invited to attend vespers and dine with the other monks. The chapel was packed with town folk attending evening prayers. Lots of reciting and chanting, a moving affair even for those who shy away from religious ceremony.

Introduced to the Abbot, Father Anton. He inquired about my pilgrimage as we moved together through ornate doors into a very large hall. Long tables were set up with plates, cups, and cutlery. Noticed that all the place sets faced a dais at the far end of the hall.

Brother Paul explained that there was to be no talking, we must eat in silence whilst a monk read from the Bible. The food was basic and nourishing. Had a long table all to myself, in front were three monks sat as far apart from each other as the spacing would allow.

Plain robes, a cross, sandals, eating only because they must – a simple life. Brother Paul said that they always made good use of their time, prayer being very important, and must continue even during meal times.

A stark contrast to regimental dinner nights; the tables laid lavishly with silver, candelabra, best crockery and finest port. We dress in full evening regalia with polished medals and indulge in exquisite delights prepared by regimental chefs consuming excellent vintages.

Are we so different? The military and the clergy are disciplined, dedicated to a cause, well organised, and follow a strict code of conduct. We have oft ventured forth hand in hand in the name of religion, conquest, riches, or peace! After all, what were the crusades all about?

There I was, in a Benedictine abbey surrounded by devoted monks; men who gave their lives to God and the Church. They'd taken vows to live in a secluded community, withdrawn from society and ate boiled cabbage everyday! This couldn't be further removed from military life, yet I could see the parallels; a shared past of conflict and conquest, of bloody invasion and exhorting Christianity to every corner of the world.

Back on the trail toward Pola de Sierro, I could make out the mountain pass I hoped to cross today. Noticed the red sign for a petrol station and promised myself an ice-cream. The petrol station pit stop had long been abandoned. There were a few houses and rusted steel signs, nothing more. The ice-cream would have to wait.

That night I slept at Pola de Sierro, finally felt like I was hitting my stride.

Day 21: Pola de Sierro to Oviedo – 23 km

Grey skies announced a glum start shrouded in a chilly fog. The Camino was generally flat and passed through shabby villages, shabby industrial estates, going over the motorway on at least four occasions. A dirty boring path to Oviedo was made never-ending by ugliness. The less said the better!

Walking three abreast! – Camino del Norte

4
Camino Primitivo

"For me there is only the travelling on paths that have heart, on any path that may have heart, and the only worthwhile challenge is to traverse its full length – and there I travel looking, looking breathlessly."

~Carlos Castaneda, The Teachings of Don Juan ~

The Original Way or Camino Primitivo was the first and most ancient of the Caminos, used by King Alfonso II to get to Santiago in the 9th century. From Oviedo to Santiago there are over 300 kilometres of rugged mountainous terrain. The food and sidra make the challenging route worthwhile. There is a Camino saying:

Quien va a Santiago
y no al Salvador
visita su criado
pero no a su Señor.

Whoever goes to Santiago
and not the Saviour,
visits the servant
and not the Lord.

In Oviedo the Cathedral of San Salvador or Holy Saviour is the start of the Camino Primitivo. This became a significant pilgrim destination in the 11th Century as it held several relics. Pilgrims on the French route would come towards Oviedo at León. Known as the Camino de San Salvador the mountain route is not well marked and few pilgrims attempt it. In 2014 it took me four days to complete – the second day was the hardest by far of any Camino I have walked. The signs were poor and high up in the mountains it is very easy to take the wrong turn and walk the wrong way for hours before discovering the mistake.

In 2011 Tammy and I completed the Camino Primitivo, walking most of the way with a group of pilgrims from all corners of Spain. Tammy was the youngest at 15, Roberto, from Toledo, the eldest at 74! Nine of us walking at our own pace ending each day at the same albergue. We continued as a group all the way to the end, Mich joining us for the final 100 km to Santiago.

Day 22: Oviedo to Cornellana – 36 km

Hoped I would remain injury free throughout the challenging Camino Primitivo. Knew this route well, how hard it was over the Asturian highlands, and where the best watering holes were. The last few days had not been easy, the substantial effort draining my energy reserves. The Camino Primitivo is one of the best walks I had completed. This was my third time through and I looked forward to the challenge.

The long urban walk out of Oviedo was boring, negotiating traffic, pedestrian crossings, and fast-paced faceless people scurrying to work. It took an hour and a bit to get to the city limits. All large cities are the same. There are many pilgrims who choose not to walk in or out, opting instead to use public transport. Fair enough! It can take up to two hours to get clear of some cities.

Had some juice and sweet pastries, sat on a bench by the side of a green-zone. Mulled over the rat race of working life. Freedom had not come easy. I had been trapped for so long

51

thinking work the most important thing. Scared of retirement, unsure of what the future would bring, I wondered how I would survive without routine. Six years later I believe that it was the best decision ever. My time was my own, not something I'd give to endeavours not of my choosing.

"You don't realise how lucky you are, being able to do what you do, having the liberty to disappear for weeks or months on end!" I was often reminded of my fortunate circumstances by my close friend and confidant, Danny Freyone. "People stop me in Main Street and ask – where's Mark? What's he up to? And I reply – gallivanting around the world, enjoying retirement!" Danny tells me.

"I envy your freedom, your ability to switch off and follow your dream, making the most of what you have." Being with Danny reminded me of my army days, a time of hyper-active living, of packing 26 hours into the day and paying little attention to my flanks – the family around me!

These last few years we'd often jump into my ageing VW T3 campervan and drive away for a few days, Matthew, Danny, and I. The army kept me from the ones I loved, but it was my choice. I adore the military, would not have changed things for the world! But, maybe, I ask myself again and again, maybe I shouldn't have obsessed so long over my career.

"Stories we tell ourselves!" Matt told me over a shared cup of wine. "We tell tall tales everyday, to sweeten the bitter ambiguity of life. Twists to the truth, lies but not quite lies you know, enough to maintain that shiny image." Had been caught in that web of wishful self imposed deceit for too long.

The Camino peels away layers of fiction in our lives allowing us to see ourselves for what we truly are. We are freed from the inhibitions accumulated during the walk of life.

This day I had a very long walk, devilish hills, rolling landscape, and ankle busting descents.

The sweltering heat and humid climate forced me to drink lots of water, resting for short breaks for my legs and feet. During such a stop I drank from a roadside fountain which seemed safe enough, refreshing my head and face.

Day 23: Cornellana to Tineo – 31 km

A sleepless night. Dashed in and out of bed with a terrible bout of the runs. Must have been the water from the fountain! My belly was churning and groaning and the volatile contents warned of impending volcanic eruption! Dozed off. Sunrise came too soon, felt exhausted and perhaps should have stayed in bed to recover.

Got some re-hydration solution from the chemist, started downing sachets of the stuff and had a late start. It was a killer march. Thought about films like They Died with Their Boots On (in my case sandals), and March or Die. I was in bits, walking today was not a good idea. The sensible option would have been to rest and recuperate. Only an unshakable stubbornness can account for my stupidity. As for the route, yep, I'm sure it was pretty. 31 never-ending kilometres on an empty fuel deposit.

In 2014 a Basque called Iñaki and Jorge from Valencia shared a good few walking days with me. They were separatists, we conversed about the royals and corruption. Iñaki disheartened with the monarchy felt cheated with the recent appointment of the new king. He had hoped the old king would be the last monarch.

Jorge told me he lived in the most corrupt region of the most corrupt country in Europe – Valencia, Spain! He blamed the closure of his fathers thriving restaurant for his premature death. "Papa was given no option. They demolished the place to make way for a railway line, pittance in compensation. Lost his business, clientele, and what he loved doing the most – cooking! He never recovered". Jorge later became a politician in the hope he could make a difference, and retired very disillusioned with the whole system.

Tineo was a sight to behold. Shattered, in pain, aching from head to toe I collapsed on my bed. I learned throughout my walks that success is achieved pasito a pasito, step by step. That night I slept like a bear in hibernation. Looking back, this was my darkest moment. It was the only day which I remember not wanting to walk, and that is precisely why I forced myself to do so.

Day 24: Tineo to Pola de Allande – 26 km

Wouldn't call it a full recovery, but was feeling much better. Set off early, uphill for three hours then a steep descent. Forced myself to eat my first bite since the dreaded night.

Came across a bar at a hamlet called Porciles, owned by Jose, a character far greater than life. Had been here in 2011 with Tammy and he had held onto the scrap of paper with my contact details. We spoke for over an hour about the Camino and Jose's participation on numerous Spanish TV shows as an extra.

I remembered my own brief brush with the acting profession. All the way back in 1983 a bunch of us from the Regiment were on a mountain climbing expedition in the Atlas Mountains near Marrakesh. We were approached and asked to be extras for a film, they said we were perfect for the part. We were military and the movie was on the Arab-Israeli War. Offered food, lodgings, and a small fee, but! We were required to die as part of the plot. "Not likely," one of the chaps said, and that was that.

A couple took the seats next to me. Pedro and Colette met 8 years ago whilst on the Camino Francés. Fell head over heels in love, they married and are the proud parents of two young girls. This, their second Camino; a romantic walking holiday in plush hotels and through good restaurants.

Known many who meet on the Camino and get hitched. Tammy still corresponds with Victor and María, who found each other on the trail in 2011 and remain together five years on.

What a delightful reunion, Jose always smiling and carefree. I ended the day at Pola de Allande. That night I managed to eat properly, I knew what lay ahead the next day; mountains and more mountains.

Day 25: Pola de Allande to Salime – 34 km

Ascending the road with a river on your left, looking up you'll see lo Alto del Palo, a mountain pass at 1146 m. Once off road the trail meanders parallel to the river for some distance, going up and up, diverging as the steep ascent begins. Getting to the highest point of this Camino is not for the faint-hearted, particularly with 10 kg on your back and in rain and cold.

A few kilometres into the days walk I passed by a middle-aged couple. She was struggling and unsure of the deteriorated wooden bridge over a small stream. He held her

Outside Jose's bar in Porciles

hand and led her across. As I passed I noticed the anguish in her face, could tell she was not at all enjoying the forced river crossing! I said hello and offered to help.

Daniel and Mariana, from Brazil, had started their Camino in Oviedo a few days earlier. They were finding it quite difficult due to the hills and rugged terrain. It was their first Camino; not a good choice for beginners. They had read Paulo Coelho's book – The Pilgrimage, which inspired them to walk. Both carrying far too much weight, most likely extra clothing and toiletries.

Their main mistake was trying to stick to the route proposed by their guide book. Whilst the distance was reasonable, they were not accustomed to walking and should have gone far less than suggested. Many pilgrims believe they will be fine because during preparation they walked 25/30 km in a day. What about walking on day 2? Day 3? 4? And the next day?

Pains, aches, blisters, lack of home comforts, and accumulative tiredness follow the first few days of the Camino. It simply isn't the same as walking the distances during training. I have seen many throw in the towel.

Got them to sit down, take their boots off, sink their feet in the cool river waters. Sat next to them and rolled up the bottom of my trousers dipping my legs in the stream. Water is such a lift to the spirit, a remedy for aching feet and legs. They couldn't believe I was walking in sandals. Told them they should try to enjoy the walk, to continue only if it pleased them. Religious or any other reasons aside the real experience in the Camino is in the journey.

Today I would ascend el Palo, reach the end of the recommended etapa, and go on to walk the next stage. Had done this last year, feeling much better than yesterday, I knew I could do it again. The views from the top of el Palo make it so the effort is not in vain. I was wet, cold, and felt drained, pushing myself up the last steep stretches to the summit pass. Took shelter in a little refuge. Needed to dry myself, change into warm clothing, and take nourishment. Stuffed wet heavy clothes into my bag and set off again.

Now for the worst bit. An agonizingly long descent, ouch! Never enjoyed downhill as it damages the ankles, knees, and hips. I often take a tumble or two during my walks, unsurprisingly, on the descent. Glad to report I didn't tumble this time.

In the village of Berducedo there is a little shop where I replenish my supplies, and much further at La Mesa a refuge. Here I stop, eat and tend to my feet. At the next summit a splendid view of the lake below, the Embalse de Salime, looking like a small emerald glimmering afar. Another brutal, very long descent through an ancient pine-tree forest. Across the dam and some distance up the road there is a little road side hotel. Tired and thirsty I decided not to push and did not reach my original target. It would have been another 7 km uphill to Grandas de Salime. No need to beast myself.

That night I met a pilgrim, an elderly lady from South Africa, who was in a very bad state. We sat at the bar and she told me about her grandchild who was at death's door. Her boots were heavy, she could walk no further. She was doing this for the dying boy. I told her to call a taxi, to go a few days ahead on the Camino, rest, and maybe she will experience a small miracle. Saw her on the approach to Santiago, cheerful and revived.

Difficult terrain and illness had made the last four days trying, had to dig deep. Now walked more than a third of the way, all going well would expect to be in Santiago de Compostela in a week.

Day 26: Embalse de Salime to Fonsagrada – 33 km

The first 7 km were uphill on tarmac roads towards the town of Grandas de Salime. It was hot and humid. Started late, aching from yesterday's exertions. Knew today would also be a long one, plenty of hills and steep roads. About three hours into the trail I stopped, had my first bite at a road-side café.

Following a steep ascent of a hill lined with wind turbines I came to a pine forest. Up through a gap in the trees, another steep climb, and on a grassy path gently downhill. At this point I was on the demarcation line between Asturias and Galicia.

Crossed the road to a wooded area, rickety fences, hedges, and endless stonewalls dividing small fields. Lush and green due to frequent rainfall, running water and oozing mud even in summer. The route through Galicia came as no surprise, hard terrain with folded land and marvellous views. Kilometres of thick forests rising steeply from crystal clear waters, every so often a stone cottage hamlet appears. Walking these mountain routes is a pleasure, my effort more than worthwhile.

In 2011 at Fonsagrada nine of us feasted on octopus and birthday cake. María, the 19 year old birthday girl, and her mother Angeles sat at the centre of the table. We all knew, except for Angeles, about María and Victor being secret sweethearts.

The days were somewhat blending into one another. I could see Fonsagrada, high up in the hills. There is a superb pulperia here which makes the most delicious pulpo a la Gallega* and served to symbolise my return to Galicia.

Day 27: Fonsagrada to O'Cadavo – 31 km

Is that, another climb I see? Yes, quite possibly the steepest section of the whole Camino Primitivo. Not too long, only about 1 km, resembling the offspring of Hole in the Wall and Rock Gun Hill (the steepest hills on the Rock of Gibraltar!). Tightened my sandal straps, took a deep breath, and stepped off to a rendition of Popcorn played out by clattering teeth; a nasty habit of mine. Mind you, I have a whole repertoire!

Passed an easy going couple and a young South Korean who said buen camino. She struggled with the hill, carrying too much weight, a camera around her neck, and all smiles. Replied buen camino cheerfully and motored on up the hill. At the top I rested, looking back down saw a small speck, slowly, deliberately crawling up the winding path. She had

*Octopus Galician style.

not abandoned, her legs moving by will power had overcome the impulse to surrender.

I was above the clouds, great white clouds streaming between trees and swirling about in the valleys between the mountain tops. Everything is in bloom, a mixture of yellow, magenta, green, and the buzz of a thousand living things.

Stopped at a little restaurant at the bottom of the long descent. Remembered the owner, an Argentine, from previous years, he did not recognise me. Asked for a thick slice of toast with olive oil, tomato, and cured ham. He insisted on bringing me a bocadillo according to the menu, which, as a special favour he could toast, the tomato as extra! I reminded him that we argued last year, and a few years earlier about just this. He tells me that what I want is a toasted sandwich, not toast with condiments! Semantics – tostada or bocadillo, I knew what to expect. Alfredo would not deviate from the menu board. I smiled and graciously accepted his offering. Felt sorry for the Germans who placed their order only to be told that they too were not ordering properly.

Day 28: O'Cadavo to Lugo – 35 km

Walking in fog with limited visibility is no fun, a chill in the air and freezing droplets drenching my clothes. Slept very well and felt much stronger than previous days. The route today was generally flat and followed wooded paths and tarmac roads. Soon the fog was pierced by light and dissipated, warmer, brighter, the start of a glorious sunny day.

Heard singing then the sound of someone running behind me, finally the salutation "halo!" Was joined by a German pilgrim on his second Camino. We stopped for coffee, chatted and walked together for the rest of the day. Conrad is from Dresden, part of what used to be the old East Germany. We had a meaningful conversation on re-unification, the Camino, and life in general.

Of great interest were his memories of East Germany under Soviet rule, how the Russian soldiers were sad when they had to return home. He recalls they'd said that though things were not well in East Germany, it was far worse in Russia. We discussed the bombing of Dresden by British and US aircraft close to the end of the Second World War. Told him of my great grandmother who had been killed during a bombing raid in the London Blitz, when a water cistern fell on her in the toilet. Conrad was experiencing difficulties in his life; separation from his partner, a young child in-between. We got to Lugo, had a beer, and went our separate ways.

Lugo is a large walled city with an interesting cathedral, large plaza, and decent albergue. In 2011 Michelle had flown to Santiago and taken the bus to Lugo where Tammy and I had met her. We had walked together, the three of us for four days. In 2014 I walked this same route from Lugo to Santiago in just two days.

Day 29: Lugo to Palas de Rei – 42 km

Started late, did not want to be caught in the snaking line of pilgrims exiting Lugo. Walking in or out of a city is rarely nice, often confusing. If you cross a major river though, provided you have a city map, you can get to the bridge without having to follow the vieras, scallop shells on the pavement. Knew where my crossing point was and thought I could ignore the marked trail.

It was rush hour, school children blocked my way and I took a left and then a right thinking, bah, this is more or less the right direction. Why, oh why did I not just pull out my city map? Chuleria, cockiness, a confidence in my navigational skills! I faced a cul-de-sac and had no choice but to perform an about turn, only to end up in another cul-de-sac. Swallowing the remnants of my pride I asked for directions and finally got to the bridge.

The walk today was mostly flat on secondary roads, passing through several very small villages. After about 15 km I came to the first bar, ordered an omelette bocadillo and a beer. Two men walked in and asked the couple behind the bar if they could set up a field kitchen on the grass outside. They prepared food for a large group of Spanish pilgrims. The next day I saw their four wheel drive speed by full of bags, kit, and a pilgrim or two.

Hours later at a second bar I was surprised to find my German friend, Conrad. He joined me for a coffee and we went on together.

The hills crept up on us, saw a large group of South Koreans on a Santiago walking holiday. Took a picture with them, of course. A bus picked them up from the top of the hill, Conrad went his own way, I moved on to finish at Palas de Rei. Had now completed the Camino Primitivo and joined the Camino Francés.

Several lamps illuminated the front room, rucksacks and other personal belongings lay strewn along the walls. The adjoining room was busy with pilgrims preparing their

South Korean pilgrims

sleeping space, tending to worn feet, resting, talking, re-packing bags, getting ready for the night routine. All eyes turned as I gave my greetings.

Showered fully dressed, had a hearty meal watching the football. Tables were full, the pilgrim menu only 10 €. Next to me an elderly French lady toyed with her food, her companion feasted on his platter and then hers.

Night was cool and rowdy, cacophony of whistling and coughs followed by a melodious staccato rendition of the pilgrims nocturnal symphony. Had heard it all before and came well prepared with ear plugs.

In 2011, at the end of the Earth – Finisterre, I had a bed bound slapping contest with a French pilgrim. We were packed like sardines in a can, fast asleep in my bunk right in the middle of dozens of snoring pilgrims. Smack! Bleary, I opened my eyes and noticed the guy next to me with a finger on his lips, shushing me! Guess my snoring was that bad, turned over and went back to sleep. Whack! Another slap! My retaliation was swift and hard, slapping him twice on the face, one for each slap he'd delivered! He cowered in his sleeping bag and that was the end of that. This guy wasn't very diplomatic. Have slept in albergues all over and put up with snoring pilgrims, but never had I experienced the impertinence of being slapped!

5
Camino Francés

"It's better to walk alone than with a crowd going in the wrong direction"

~Diane Grant, playwright and screenwriter~

The Camino Francés, the route most people refer to when they talk about the Camino de Santiago. It is the most frequented, over 70% of pilgrims registering at the Pilgrim Office in Santiago have walked on the Camino Francés, and 50% of those begin at Sarria, 112 km from Santiago.

100 km is the minimum distance required to officially obtain the Compostela. I walked with the flow of pilgrims at a steady pace on a generally gentle route. During the last Holy Year in 2010 over 189,000 pilgrims walked the Camino Francés.[*]

Day 30: Palas de Rei to Arzúa – 29 km

Started the day with a cheese & ham croissant. Relaxing in a shaded area contemplating passing pilgrims when my phone started blurting an infernal melody. The Commanding Officer Ivor Lopez greeted me heartily. I was sitting down having a break, in no danger of walking in the wrong direction. Ivor chuckled and asked how I was. "Sweaty and dirty," I said, to which he replied "You know there are showers in Spain, don't you?" Very funny. I step into the shower wearing my clothes every day as it saves time, and soap!

*Statistics from the Pilgrim Office in Santiago.

Ivor has often mentioned that his biggest regret was not joining me for the adventure training phase of our Canada deployment; Exercise Medicine Man. Following a gruelling three weeks on the prairies of British Columbia, during which we only had one shower (without clothes!), I was selected as Battlegroup Adventure Training Officer.

It was too cold for rafting, parachuting had been cancelled. We went cross-country skiing for a week, lived out in snow-holes, climbed Mount Athabasca, 3491 m, towering above the Columbia Icefield and were taught crevasse rescue drills. This was all the way back in 1993, I was a fresh faced Captain, only 30!

Ivor said that Adie O'Shea had shared in the gruelling experience, most likely the reason he hadn't walked with me in the UK. OK Ivor, was it really that bad?

Got to Arzúa where I spent the night at Casa Teodora. I knew the owners, two brothers, Gabriel and David, often staying there. Today I drank too much coffee, stopped too many times! It rained for most of the day.

Day 31: Arzúa to Lavacolla – 27 km

Yet another late start with many pilgrims on the trail. Yesterday I saw five pilgrims get taxis, and more on buses. Inclement weather does that, today I saw more doing the same close to Santiago!

There are many types of pilgrims, most are not used to walking. To their credit they suffer the hardships of attempting to walk with wrong types of footwear, too many clothes, and enormous rucksacks. There are some very large groups of foreign peregrinos-turisticos, tourist pilgrims, with no rucksacks, supported by a travel agent or with a guide.

Each Camino is different and all are valid. I stop 10 km from Santiago at Lavacolla, never stopped so near before. Michelle gets to Santiago tomorrow. Thought why not halt here rather than spending the extra night alone in Compostela.

Observed the changes in the land with growing anticipation. Felt relaxed and ready for a good break. The previous evening at Casa Teodora, having a drink with Gabriel and one of the waiters, Manolo, said;

"Spain is not a country. It is many different countries, many different people with different languages. Galicia is different to Castilla y León, which is different to Andalucía. The demarcation of regions is more than a matter of physical geography."

Today I passed through O Pedrouzo. Here on the 12th July 2011 we celebrated our 25th wedding anniversary. We splashed out, ate and drank with our Camino friends. The next morning Mich and I hiked up to Monte do Gozo, Mount Joy, where we met Antonio and Maricarmen. Antonio had left the group days earlier to pick up Maricarmen, a multiple sclerosis sufferer. A surprise appearance close to the end! She managed to walk the final 5 km to Santiago.

Day 32: Lavacolla to Santiago – 10 km

Woke up, packed my dirty kit, left. Past the Galicia TV station, the brewery, the camping round the corner, stopped and had a coffee and the best Torta de Santiago* ever! Dozens of pilgrims taking a break and milling around the souvenir stall. Monte do Gozo took the photo, stamped my credentials, sat and had another coffee. Pilgrims often hang

---

*An almond cake with a cross.

around here contemplating their walk and impending arrival at the main square in front of the cathedral.

Santiago!

Through the stone archway over cobbled flagstones, you are at the Praza do Obradoiro, on your right the Parador Los Reyes Catolicos.* I sat for a very long time between the arches of the Galician Parliament and admired the cathedral. A cacophony of noise of metal pointed sticks against stone, the piper playing his looping melodic tune, the cathedral bells chiming the hour, a chatter of tourists wearing raincoats. I had arrived at Santiago de Compostela. The bones of St James were just there, in the crypt below the main altar of the cathedral.

The church seemed to emanate an aura of solitude, of serenity, tranquillity. Detail of the stonework, the majesty of the façade compelled attentive study. The serenity directly contrasted by the mass of humanity circling the praza where pilgrims converged from all the Caminos. Following weeks of suffering and hardships, culminating all in the arrival at this very spot in the shadows of the towers of the cathedral. Groups of pilgrims and tourists of all ages, embracing, rejoicing, kissing each other, and prostrating to kiss the cobbles.

Entered the cathedral, climbed the stairs behind the altar, embraced the back of the statue of the apostle, descended into the crypt to view the tomb of St James. The ritual, complete.

*Hotel of the Catholic Kings. Paradores are found throughout Spain and often are castles, monasteries, or other historical buildings.

Days 33/34: Santiago de Compostela

I am not at the end of my Walk to the Rock, not even halfway! Not emotional, not rejoicing, not on a pilgrimage. But, very satisfied with my progress. Tonight I shall take on the Paris-Dakar! A real challenge – running the gauntlet of bars frequented by pilgrims; at one extreme the bar O Paris, at the other end bar Café Bar Dakar.

This was the hardest phase yet. The Camino Primitivo is very challenging, not for those who are not prepared for the long distances over mountainous terrain.

Most who walk this route are seasoned pilgrims, a few who are on their first Camino too often quit. I was disappointed at the number using taxis and buses to complete the etapas, or who just cut out a stage entirely. For some it's acceptable, due to their more advanced age, others could have had a better time walking elsewhere. Each to his own.

I had been in Santiago many times, often it would be the end of my journey. Now it was time for the real challenge, nothing to it Mark, pick yourself up and go!

Day 35: Santiago de Compostela to Arzúa – 37 km

Departed early making my way through the narrow streets of the casco antiguo. The medieval streets which were bustling just a few hours earlier now silent. They surely lay in bed, recovering from running the gauntlet of the Paris-Dakar! I felt strong, rejuvenated by my weekend break. Michelle was tucked away in bed back at the hotel, knew she never enjoyed our partings so asked her not to accompany me out of the city. Soon I was back up the Monte do Gozo, next Lavacolla, on the track past the airport. Thought about

Santiago de Compostela – Praza do Obradoiro

Mich as I passed the periphery of the fenced runway, knowing she now would be preparing for her flight home.

Advanced against the human tide of pilgrims. Most greeted me, some looked, a few stopped and asked a question or two. The odd one joked that I was heading in the wrong direction, pointed towards Santiago laughing. This continued all day. I began counting pilgrims as one does sheep to try to sleep.

At a pilgrim filled bar I stopped for a break. Bought a beer and slice of tuna empanada.* Whilst many walk on their own the majority walk in pairs or groups. Two Italian pilgrims smiled and asked where I was heading to today. When I replied Arzúa they were baffled and inquisitive. Explained what I was doing and they turned to talk to someone else.

Got to Arzúa in good time, to Casa Teodora and greeted Gabriel – one of the brothers who owned and managed the establishment. Every time I stayed he would join me for a glass of tinto, and discuss his business. Entirely dependent on the passage of pilgrims, it is a profitable seasonal affair with a heavy workload from May to September, slow uptake in between. They own a second albergue and restaurant and are always busy during walking season. We had often talked about Gibraltar and the tourist industry, he was astonished to learn that millions visit the Rock every year.

Day 36: Arzúa to Ventas de Narón – 39 km

There were pilgrims every step of the way, most on their own, many in groups, some moving faster than others. I walked and allowed my senses to take it all in, slowly assimilating the vision of hundreds of people of all ages and types walking with one purpose, with one thought; getting to

*Pastry turnover with savoury fillings, baked or fried.

Santiago. Felt like a salmon forcing my way upstream. There must be a million different reasons for walking a pilgrimage, I'd met my fair share of pilgrims over the years, each with a unique purpose. How I wish I could read minds, listen to each of their stories, or be a fly on the wall of an albergue.

There were another 13 km to push, by the end it seemed so much longer. The kilometres on the mojones, marker stones, did not tally with my information. According to the markers I had walked over 40 km. Well, in the end I got there – starving! A substantial plate of lentil soup followed by bacon, eggs and chips, washed down by a glass of a spicy red, did the trick.

Something that conspired to make the day longer was the number of times I was stopped and asked why I was going the wrong way! The plus side was meeting some interesting people and chatting with them.

At the entrance to a village I met a Mexican family from Monterrey, who had also set off from Sarria. They were sat by a typical lavadero* fed by water from a stream. Took my rucksack off and without hesitation dipped my sandalled feet into the water. They gawked, I convinced them to remove their boots and do the same. They wore thick woolly socks, oh dear!

There we were, five pilgrims sharing the lavadero, watching others pass by. My newly found Mexican friends were very much enjoying the moment.

Met another long distance walker, Carla from South Africa. She began way back in mid-March from Rome and was taking it easy. When she got to France, tired of walking, she bought a bicycle and rode it 900 km. Carla was a few days from Santiago, intending to go on to Finisterre and Muxía.

*An old outdoor wash-room from a time gone past.

She reckoned she would have travelled some 3000 km in total.

Carla was a free spirit, lost and later found a personal religion. Stood by the side of the trail and exchanged views of our Caminos for an hour as pilgrims passed in droves. In no hurry, nowhere we needed to be, understood the joy and significance of living the moment.

Later I was stopped by a friendly Polish couple. He said I looked like Chuck Norris, nice!

The surprise encounter of the day was seeing a cheerful happy going couple, Daniel and Mariana! After we went our separate ways at the Alto del Palo on day 25 they worked together and overcame their difficulties. Thoroughly enjoying their adventure, Mariana gave me a kiss on the cheek, Daniel gave me a huge hug. A truly joyful reunion, "obrigado, buen camino peregrinos".

Day 37: Ventas de Narón to Sarria – 36 km

Started later than usual, suffering the effects of yesterday's long haul. Scenic views and cool breeze getting slowly warmer. So many, many pilgrims on the Camino, lost count after 600! Got to Portomarín in good time, bought some cured ham, cheese, bread, and juice; my sustenance for the day. Had brunch, saved some for later and pushed on.

Met an old lady having a rough time coming down a dangerously steep hill as I slogged up. She was scared, hurting from the strain on her ankles and knees. She accepted my offer to take her by the arm and help her down safely. Glanced back as I plodded up the same hill a second time; she would be fine. Didn't get her name or nationality, felt happy that I could be of some help.

A tiredness crept over me, felt as if a brick had been put in my rucksack, and trust me – I knew exactly how this felt! Something we regularly used to do in the military was carry extra weight, often in the form of bricks, on our forced marches and runs. One time, when waiting to board a military aircraft to the UK, I weighed my kit at the RAF hangar in Gibraltar and found it unusually heavy. Added it to the pile of bags and forgot all about it.

At the other end I struggled with my rucksack, hauling it into my room I unpacked a collection of bricks, tin cans, and empty gun-shells! What could I do? Accept defeat at the hands of my soldiers? St Martin's Plain Camp, Folkstone in the winter is awful cold. 0600 hrs, got the troops up for a nice refreshing early morning run. The culprits – most likely Corporals Lopez, Coleing, or maybe the Duarte twins, all looked at me with nothing to say. Revenge is a dish best served fast, and on big plates!

Avoided eye contact with most pilgrims as I didn't fancy stopping much today. Many pointed the way to Santiago for me, funny the first time. Saw a group of pilgrims on horseback scattering walkers as they sauntered through. Had a chat with an elderly local lady herding cattle with three Alsatians and a whipping stick, which she put to good effect! She had been to Gibraltar on a coach trip and enjoyed it. Sarria, stopped for the night – this is the start point for the majority of pilgrims on their way to Santiago.

Walking against the flow of pilgrims – Camino Francés

Horses on the pilgrim trail to Santiago

Day 38: Sarria to Alto do Poio – 34 km

Left Sarria heading towards Pontin, made good time. Felt an excruciating pain on my right Achilles tendon, continued to climb hill after hill focusing on the road ahead. Right foot tightly strapped with an ankle support, pain did not subside. Considered halting for the day, concerned that if this went on it would affect my walk. Any type of foot injury at this stage would be disastrous. My fears of failure resurfaced. I now felt stronger, confident, there was nothing to it – had to keep on going.

About 6 km from Tricastela I came upon a cascade of water emptying into a tranquil pool. Stuck my feet in till they went numb. The water was cold, invigorating, let my mind wonder and relaxed, the ideal spot! Small miracles happen on the Camino. The pain disappeared as quickly as it arrived. Took out a blueberry muffin, took a bite, and with exquisite butter fingers dropped it into the pool of clear water. The muffin was carried away and flowed half submerged further and further beyond my reach. The cascade demanded payment for its curative effect, taking half my muffin!

Got to Tricastela and bought food and drink, some of which I reserved for later. There were pilgrims stopped for the day hanging around bars, doing what pilgrims do best, drink! Ascended the steep hill out of town to the mountains, saw more pilgrims approaching the end of their day's walk.

Brutal hill climb up to lo Alto do Poio, clenched my fists, gripped my poles unwilling to accept defeat; I would not be beaten by this hill! Saw fellow pilgrims descend the steep slope, knew the downhill was no joy. Passed hamlet after hamlet on a winding mountain road.

When the route appeared to be getting lenient, it got steeper. Blistering hot, mouth dry, consumed copious amounts of water but could not quench my thirst. Getting very frustrated with the whole thing. I moaned, groaned, mumbled my thoughts aloud. Maybe it was the wine speaking, raised my right arm towards the commanding mountainous features and, imitating Roman gladiators exclaimed "those who are about to die salute you!"*

---

*Entirely historically accurate (!) as depicted in the documentary film Gladiator.

Hard as it was I moved at a steady pace. Plenty of stops and drinks ensured good time to the Alto do Poio, 1335 m. Stopped for refreshment, called ahead for accommodation. Alas, there wasn't an empty bed to be found at O Cebreiro so I grabbed the last remaining room at the Posada del Peregrino. 8 km short of O Cebreiro, in for a longer walk tomorrow.

By the time I went for supper the dining room was booming with pilgrims. Settled on the only vacant seat at the end of the table, to my left Geoff from Ireland, next to him Paul who was Dutch, on my right an Aussie – John, and Laura from Brazil. The four met on the walk and were talkative. Being two courses behind them, I was more in listening mode rather than participating in their discussions.

Geoff was friendly and funny, cracking jokes. Paul and John spoke seven languages between them. They talked about their walk, distances travelled, difficulties on the road. Asked a lot of questions which I didn't reply to, just kept nodding my head. Food arrived – comida casera, delightful home made fare.

Geoff said this was his second time on the Camino, only walking a section previously and never reaching Santiago, now trying to complete. He was having difficulty with his feet, you guessed it, boots again! The others were on their first attempt, commencing at different places. They were astonished to discover that I started in Cardiff and had now walked over 1000 km in sandals.

The mood in the dining room was contagious with over thirty people speaking at the same time. This was pilgrim territory, their favourite nocturnal pastime; celebrating the day's efforts over a meal and bottle of wine. Conversations played out concurrently the length of the long table. An Italian pilgrim approached our end and asked John for some wine, snatching the bottle from in front of me. John warned it was not his to give. I grabbed the pilgrim's hand and said, "if you want my wine you should ask, not take what isn't yours".

Alarmed by my reaction he withdrew with an empty cup. When the Italian sat I instructed John to pour him some wine, he waved at me in gratitude.

Paul sat next to me and whispered in my ear. He said that Laura had three nasty blisters on the same foot and if I minded fixing them. She was in considerable pain and preferred to let the blisters be. I explained that if she was going to continue she should have them seen to. None of them quite knew how to deal with blisters, only Paul was willing to learn.

Got out my highly sophisticated 'surgical' instruments; needle and thread. Sterilized my tools and lanced the blisters, run thread through, spraying some povidone, iodine antiseptic, on the exposed area. Tied the thread to keep the blister open and allow it to drain and dry. Laura squinted every time I pierced a swollen fluid filled bubble on the surface of her skin.

I ordered four HIJOPUTA's,* chupitos de crema de orujo,+ and knew we were in for a long night! The real Camino is what you find on the way, pilgrims and the stories we all have to tell.

Day 39: Alto do Poio to Camponaraya – 52 km

8 km short of my target yesterday, on the trail at the crack of dawn. Would have to play catch up. Foggy and chilly, I wore my down feather jacket. Before reaching O Cebreiro I

*Son of a bitch, a brand of the drink orujo.
+A strong liqueur similar to Irish cream.

encountered many pilgrims on narrow paths connecting the numerous hamlets on this mountainous section of the Camino. A thick mist covered everything except for the high peaks which framed the horizon. Visibility poor, the chill made it pleasantly cold, a welcome change to yesterday. Whilst I had walked this twice before this was the first time in reverse. At the Alto de San Roque, 1270 m, took some photos of the large statue of the pilgrim, today it appeared to be struggling in the fog.

Got to O Cebreiro walking generally downhill except the final section. Covered the 8 km in good time, an hour and thirty-five minutes. Approached the town on the track through pine woodland and remembered the last time I had been here.

It was in July of 2013 when Tammy and I spent a wonderful evening at O Cebreiro. There had been as many pilgrims then as there must have been last night – every bed taken, every table at every restaurant occupied. People spilling over onto narrow cobbled streets, bottle in hand, sitting where they could. Singing, strumming guitars, making sound with other strange instruments, and rejoicing like every good pilgrim should! We sat outside, sipped hot chocolate and stargazed.

There is a special something about this place. It is the first settlement in Galicia for pilgrims on the French Way. A compulsory stop for most, a spiritual centre with cosmic significance, more than a picturesque mountain village. For many it becomes the highlight of their Camino. Two years ago Tammy and I joined the pilgrims in rejoicing and celebrating our passage through this magical spot.

This time I breakfasted at the edge of the village, overlooking the mountains and pilgrim watching. For those arriving here for the first time the stone-walled thatched roofed buildings, cobbled streets, and morning quietude could be a heavy draught. I moved down towards Castilla y León, a thousand eyes on me.

The next 12 km were down hill to Vega de Valcarce. Descended at a blistering pace ever against the steady flow of pilgrims, many struggling up the hill. Couldn't help feel sorry for them – I'd suffered that hill myself!

Oh no, a fork in the road. No visible arrows, no indications, footprints coming and going both directions. Where was that pilgrim horde when needed? Took a deep breath and entrusted myself to instinct . . . left! A steep descent on a muddy track, ah, this seems familiar, right? Fifteen minutes in I had convinced myself this was the correct path, venturing deeper and deeper into blunder valley. Finally realised my mistake, and proceeded to make an even greater one! A part of me said turn around Mark, go back now. The other, much louder voice said go on! Take the risk, no retreat!

At the bottom of a steep river valley I waded waist deep through fast flowing water, scrambled up the muddy bank covered in dirt looking like Arnie in Predator. Cut my way through thicket, slashing this way and that with my walking pole.

Pushing up through chest high scrub I came to a steep incline, wrapped in lianas and unable to go forward. Did not want to go back. You have to understand, once I commit my ingrained bone deep stubbornness takes over. Removing my rucksack I managed to edge my way on, hauling myself up on thorny thickets and scrambling on all fours. Been here before, right, just like jungle hiking round Mount Kenya – a piece of piss! Wake up Mark, you're not getting any younger! Go back! Stick to the plan!

Knew there was a road up ahead; engine noises a dead give-away. Under a fallen fence, over the rusted barbed wire, finally, the road! Dirty, tired, thorns in my arms, deep grazes on my legs, torn shirt, scratch on my nose, bruised pride, worst of all – I'd lost my second hat, my first MIA in the UK.

Lesson of the day – throw your instinct out of the window, stick to the marked path!

Following this debacle the next section was the most boring 18 km of all the Caminos; a flat road all the way to Villafranca del Bierzo.

Took a break and should have stayed, it was my intended stop. Full of beans, in marching mode, good to go for a big one. The next 13½ km dragged over undulating terrain, felt the pinch but was committed. Stopped for a beer, later a coffee, continued onward. Eventually got to Camponaraya, late and very tired, went to bed without supper.

Day 40: Camponaraya to Rabanal – 42 km

Felt surprisingly well after yesterday, no set notion of where I would end. Dawn, packed and ready to go, maybe 25 km to Acebo. A good pace, kept rhythm till Ponferrada, which has one of the best preserved Templar castles. No hanging around! Kept on going, reached Molinaseca and bought my third hat. From here it's all up hill.

Got to Acebo in four hours, still early, decided to push on. This area is el Bierzo, another mountainous section. A few kilometres past Acebo the Camino cuts across a road. Observed a number of pilgrims who appeared to be searching the area. Two men from Protección Civil* arrived in a 4-wheel drive with flashing lights and joined the search. There was a sense of urgency in the air. A pilgrim had been separated from her group who, concerned for her

*Civil Protection – organisation which assists in emergencies and disasters.

whereabouts, asked for help in searching the paths and trails nearby.

British and international papers were running a story on the disappearance of a US woman a few months earlier, her last recorded sighting near Astorga. Female pilgrims were advised not to walk alone across the Bierzo mountain range between Astorga and Ponferrada. Incidents involving sexual harassment towards women out walking and jogging in the area had been reported by the press.

This missing pilgrim, an Italian woman, had gone ahead of her friends, believing the others were in front of her. Later I heard she was found, safe and sound.

Every so often on the Camino there is a cross, maybe with a photograph, adorned with flowers, poems, messages and postcards of saints left by fellow pilgrims. Where a pilgrim had fallen there would be an epitaph. For the US woman who disappeared there was no cross, no epitaph, not when I passed through. She had vanished from the face of the earth, missing now for two months.

During my next stop I sat down with the guys from Protección Civil. They explained that the whole area was under police observation, hoping to stave off any potential threat against female pilgrims. Rumours were that the US pilgrim was abducted by an Eastern European human trafficking gang. Uniformed and undercover police took note of all suspicious activity, including car licence plates.

Encountered a pilgrim by a fountain who smiled and immediately begun talking. After a few questions about the Camino I'd guessed she was an undercover police woman, asked, and she readily confirmed.

Manjarín. Tomás, who calls himself the last Templar, has a little hideaway here serving as a rest area and albergue for those who spend the night out at the top of the mountain. By the road over a dozen sign-posts indicate distances to places like London, New York, Timbuktu.

The Cruz de Ferro, Iron Cross at 1504 m. Pilgrims place a stone which they've carried from the beginning of their walk here. This can be a very emotional moment, many look forward to finally laying down their offering. Leaving the stone by the cross has a deep-rooted symbolic significance, that of shedding weight, ridding yourself of a personal burden. Attitudes change, miraculously so, from this point on they feel born anew. Some choose to leave photographs, poems, even shoes, books, or ribbons and flags tied to the cross.

Saw cyclists at the foot of the cross taking group photos, at the parking opposite was their support vehicle. This is the highest point of the Camino Francés. Stopped for a while, rubbed some ointment on my feet, departed. Went past Foncebadón and arrived at Rabanal del Camino. Tammy would be arriving in Astorga the next day.

Day 41: Rabanal to Astorga – 20 km

A scenic gentle downhill stroll, after the past week it seemed as if I was floating along the path. The stream of pilgrims heading to Santiago persisted throughout the hot day. Could tell this affected some, many were stopped resting on their walking sticks.

A campesino* stretched out under a tree in the shade chewing tobacco, cheerily greeting all who passed. Sat next to him and rested my weary bones. Alejandro introduced himself with a black-tooth grin. He lived all his life in El

*Peasant or person living In a rural area.

Ganso, offered a little wine from his bota,* I took a swig and lay back. Proud of his children, grand children, his heritage – he loved el Bierzo, the peaceful way of life. He adored the Camino, embraced the passage of pilgrims bringing life to the area. It was terrible, he said, the disappearance of the pilgrim.

Stood and walked on, enamoured with the natural beauty, slowed down, let my mind and senses wander over the rolling hills. I walked a path of discovery, lost in thought and felt entirely immersed in the journey. In that state I remember feeling a sadness, a strange juxtaposition of emotion, empathy for the missing pilgrim, but elated to continue on the trail.

In September I heard that the remains of Denise Pikka Thiem, the missing American, were found very close to the Camino. I had drank wine, rested, and felt a peace in a place close to where she strayed from the path following a false trail of arrows. A local man was arrested in connection with her murder.

I know I will walk through that place again, Denise will be in my thoughts and I'm certain the thoughts and prayers of every pilgrim that passes by. Next time, I will look out for her epitaph.

Came to rest at an eatery in Murias de Rechivaldo. There were bars and restaurants catering to pilgrims on both sides of the street. Sat at the last place exiting the town on the road to Astorga. The silver haired lady was attending another pilgrim who complained loudly about the service. She had a taxi waiting to whisk her away to the next location and riled on about the size of her portion, the quality of the food, and

*Wineskin.

finally the cost of what she'd asked for! Gloria, the silver haired proprietress, remained quiet.

Gloria brought my dish and sat next to me. She was an experienced pilgrim and a follower of the New Age movement of the 1970's. We spoke about people, humanity, wars, spirituality, and religion. Discussed the Camino, healthy eating, and much more. Spent a good hour listening to her emotive views, interjecting every so often. The previous customer had struck a wrong chord and it appeared that Gloria wanted just to let off a little steam.

Gloria closed shop early, she had volunteered to take an elderly woman to hospital in León. A sensitive creature, she hugged and kissed me on both cheeks saying this would help make the world a better place.

Continuing I felt a strong sense of love for my fellow pilgrims, love for Denise, for Alejandro, and for Gloria. A connection, a togetherness forged through shared hardships. Walked in a state of peace, at ease with myself and the world. If you are not able to love what you are, how can you love others?

Got to Astorga, settled down and had a long siesta. Tammy arrived by the late train that night.

Day 42: Astorga

Astorga is at the far end of la Vía de la Plata, the route that will take me all the way south to Seville. La Vía de la Plata is so named because the Romans built a road for the trade of precious metals. Some argue the name is a derivative of the Arabic word ba-la-ta, meaning cobbled path.

A city with marvellous architecture and an impressive Episcopal Palace by Gaudi, lively with the constant movement of pilgrims and tourists.

We crossed the city to the south exit, scouting our route for tomorrow. Saw movement ahead coming towards us on the carretera nacional.[*] Two pilgrims, a Spaniard and a German, coming from Seville were glad to be in Astorga. They continued to journey onwards on the route I had just walked.

"Dad, the last time we were here we walked 50 km all the way from León and your sandals broke, remember?"

In the summer of 2013 we spent a night in León, in the Barrio Húmedo, the old part of the city. This sector is famous throughout Spain for the huge amount of bars, clubs, and the variety of tapas to be found. It was a long night!

With no particular thought on final destination we had set off the next morning at a comfortable pace until, snap! I faced the worst possible scenario – a sandal strap broke – disaster! No spare in the bag, resorted to tie my straps with a bit of string. No good. Wrapped my ankle support around the bottom of my sandal, fastening the Velcro strap tight on my foot, worked a treat! With every step the strap wore down, I required frequent short breaks to adjust and tighten the bindings.

After a few hours arrived at Hospital de Órbigo. Here in medieval times a knight once stood in the centre of the long bridge known as el Puente del Paso Honroso (Honourable Passage) and for a month challenged all who wished to cross to combat! If they didn't fight they would be forced to leave a glove as a sign of cowardice and wade across the river. Did not need such an excuse to wade in the cool water, my broken sandal pinched awfully.

*National road or highway.

I remember we climbed a dusty rocky trail, my sandal taking considerable punishment. At La Casa de los Dioses, David Vidal was there to help all pilgrims alike, providing food, refreshment, and assistance in any way possible. He presented me with a pair of sports shoes, 2 sizes too big. Grateful, I took them and we left.

That year Astorga was in full swing, a historical reenactment of a battle between Moros y Cristianos. We were met by Erasmo from Rome, Juan from Las Canarias, and Mike from Texas. They were amazed we had walked 50 km to catch up with them, broken sandals and all.

The next two days saw us over la Cruz de Ferro and on to Ponferrada. By then I had gifted David's sports shoes to another pilgrim and continued on snapped straps and all. Finally, at Ponferrada, I was able to find a suitable pair of new sandals.

"Yes," I said to Tammy. "I remember it well. Wearing broken sandals for 3 days was no fun!"

The French Way complete, some 260 km in reverse, 7 days of considerable effort. A strange experience, very different walking against the flow of a multitude of pilgrims. They stop to ask the same question over and over, making the same jokes – hey! Santiago is that a-ways!

Astorga – Tammy all packed!

6

La Vía de la Plata

"Energy and persistence conquer all things."

~Benjamin Franklin~

La Vía de la Plata begins in Seville and goes north through Andalucía, Extremadura and Castilla y León ending in Astorga. In 2010 the last Año Jacobeo or Holy Year; when the birthday of St James – 25th July, coincides with a Sunday, Tammy and I cycled.

That time we did not go through Astorga, taking instead the trail west through Puebla de Sanabria and Ourense. It is long, lacks infrastructure, and on occasions difficult to follow. The Carretera Nacional 630 runs along the Camino for most of the way to Seville but diverges towards Plasencia before joining up again with the main route.

In 2010 our first few days were the worst. We were unaccustomed to our bicycles, the incapacitating heat draining our enthusiasm. Packed our kit, studied the map, got on our bikes and put the pedal to the metal. Tammy reminded me that I had made her promise never to allow me to walk this. We were now about to launch ourselves on the same route in reverse towards the summer and heat!

The original Vía de la Plata was a Roman road, running in more or less a straight south-north line from Mérida to Gijón. Anyone walking this route to Santiago today will be very much aware of being in Roman Hispania. There are extended tracts of original paved road, innumerable arched bridges, milestones, and some impressive architectural ruins all along the way.

Somewhere to my south-east two friends walked diagonally across from Alicante and would cross La Vía de la Plata at some point. Sadly, I would not get to meet these Camino veterans – Bobby and Ana María Gomez, till September at a civic medal presentation ceremony in Gibraltar.

Day 43: Astorga to La Bañeza – 27 km

Dreamt I was in a salsa club. 0600 hrs and Tammy's alarm woke me up to Latino dance rhythm. On the road by 0700 hrs, we would target a shorter distance – thought it prudent to acclimatize on her first day. Carried about 6 litres of water, by mid morning it was hot. This would definitely be a trial run for what to expect further south.

Saw no pilgrims, only one or two yellow arrows, generally flat as we marched on the hard shoulder of the Nacional VI. Terrain monotonous, we had a lot to catch up on. Couldn't help but think that for most of this route to come I would be on my own.

Over the next days we spoke about university, argued politics, discussed anything and everything. Lost myself in good conversation, long distances melted away. Hardships shared are hardships halved, the Camino we were sharing was made light.

A lack of pilgrims, markings, and walking the opposite direction made it difficult to follow, or at times to find the Camino. Got to La Bañeza mid afternoon, feet hot and sore from tarmac. After washing we applied a generous amount of Vicks VapoRub.

At a bar in the town plaza I ordered a cup of their best wine. Taking the glass of red to my lips I imbibed, at once spitting the disgusting fluid back out. This vile slush, the waitress assured me, was their top wine. I shrunk back in disappointment, said this would not do. She replaced the drink with more plonk, we left without paying.

A nightmare haunted my dreams that night – the bodegas of the south had dried up, all I could find to drink was a horrid red bile...

Day 44: La Bañeza to Benavente – 39 km

The alarm was not salsa but still didn't like it. Neither did I like being forced to eat a banana and an apple at 0630 hrs, my first fruit in many days! Like mother like daughter, eh? The route, mostly road, straight as far as could see. Galloped the first 10 km and stopped for a break.

1200 hrs, stopped again at a bar, now over 20 km. Re-hydrated, had a slice of potato tortilla. It now was hot hot hot, kept on going. Noticed a long agricultural irrigation system on wheels watering crops close to the road. Looked at the sprinklers showering the field intently. What a waste, what an opportunity!

Tammy saw the look in my face and said "no, no way!" Dropped my pack and got under the sprinklers. "Come on! Venga!" No one saw us shower by the side of the road. Wet and happy from the refreshing waters we laughed, got back in step and found our rhythm once more.

Arrived at Pobladura del Valle. At the entrance were numerous underground bodegas, cellars, covered with a mound of earth, resembling something like a hobbit-hole. Having a fair distance left to walk we settled for a drink and snacks. So cool inside that we didn't want to leave. Tapas were mouth-watering, would have both been happy there all day eating and drinking!

Rubber melted between the cracks in the tarmac. Could see hazy lines rising from the sticky road. Started the day with 3 litres of water each, drank lots during stops, needed the extra fluid. Final leg of 13 km dragged on, but we persevered. Tammy understood that yesterday we walked less than 30 km and I had a schedule to keep.

Benavente at 1830 hrs, inquired about a place to stay, advised to avoid the centre of town at all costs; was the fiesta. That night the bulls would be roaming the streets. Eager spectators from all around had come and the party would go on till the early hours. We walked to the edge of town finding a decent place in the industrial zone close to the motorway.

The town was in full swing, celebrating la Fiesta del Toro Enmaromado. A bull tied by the horns is pulled through the streets whilst hundreds of brave machos Ibericos* badger the creature. Lucky we found any accommodation, Benavente was bursting to the seams.

In July of 2013, during our last joint walk on the Camino Francés, we found ourselves passing through Pamplona on the first day of the feast of San Fermín. It must have been mid morning, didn't linger long as the streets were filling up. Ascending the hill leading towards the Monte del Perdón, Mount Forgiveness, we heard the initial pyrotechnic, el Chupinazo, signal the start of la fiesta. It was 1220 hrs and twenty minutes late – a Basque flag had been hoisted illegally in la Plaza del Ayuntamiento+ and delayed proceedings. Never seen on TV were the hundreds of Basque flags adorning balconies, outside shops, bars, together with posters clamouring for Basque independence. All that we saw were bulls running through the streets.

*Males from Iberia.
+Town Hall Square.

That day in Pamplona, Mike, the Texan who had met us in Astorga, woke in the park to find his rucksack with most of his kit gone.

Day 45: Benavente to Fontanillas del Castro – 36 km

Took the initiative and switched of Tammy's phone before the alarm began to spit out some other ghastly Latino rhythm. No more unsavoury tunes to wake up to. Tammy arose to the glorious sound of bagpipes blaring Cock of the North. Game over! Up at silly hour and soon on the road. Departure drills are slick, wash, pack, good to go, brekkie some two hours into the walk.

The first 10 km followed the Camino through a sugar processing plant with huge silos, along a river, and across a disused railway bridge. Noticed the yellow arrows on a railway track, passed through cultivated fields watered by a system of irrigation, la seca. Elevated man-made canals, these channels on stilts, run for long distances delivering water where required. We often stopped and dipped our feet into the lower channels.

Soon we were on tarmac again, hours of empty roads, no hope of a venta. Walked and talked and much later found ourselves a small village with a bar on la Nacional 630. Clouds gave us much appreciated cover from the sun, a gentle breeze at our backs, the walk all the more pleasant. By 1300 hrs it was sweltering, continued to walk, drinking lots of water all the way to Fontanillas del Castro.

The town was abandoned, we were searching for the albergue and Tammy noticed a man getting out of a car and scuttling indoors. Asked about accommodation, Alfonso was very kind, insisting in helping looking for the keys to the albergue. We knocked, no one there. Next he took us to a petrol station outside town where Alfonso was sure the caretaker would be. The caretaker folded his hand of cards and took us to the albergue – a disused school hall with very limited facilities. The village had maybe 60 people, no one had been born here for years.

That night distant thunder kept me from sleep. Lying in bed sticky and uncomfortable, did not rest well. There were four beds, shower, and toilet. In the middle of nowhere, raining, sweating from every pore and sleep would not come. At the bottom bed of adjacent double-bunks Tammy slept unperturbed.

Day 46: Fontanillas del Castro to Zamora – 34 km

O630 hrs, hit the road. Tammy had a terrible heat rash on her arms and legs. I was eaten alive with flea bites the size of golf balls on my limbs, well, big. Tammy scolded me for making myself bleed from scratching.

The first 13 km were hard road till Montamarta. Breakfast, scratched some more, Tammy slapped my hand – a tendency inherited from my slap happy mother. Followed the Camino over country tracks across agricultural land.

Our last day together. This September she would be moving to Brussels to continue her studies in International Relations and French. Discussed packing her flat in Exeter, getting to Brussels, her new accommodation, Belgian beer, and mussels and chips, you know – the vital stuff!

No shade to be found amidst the flat open fields. Refreshed ourselves, pouring water over our heads, wishing in vain for another irrigation system. Got to Roales del Pan, 12 km. 7 km further and we were in Zamora, the River Duero winding through the lowlands.

Zamora has an impressive casco antiguo and is the city with the most Romanesque churches in Europe, more than I cared to count! Very tired, the heat had taken its toll.

Bars were full of locals, the selection and quality of tapas, divine! Felt bad for Tammy, she has suffered heat, road, dust, sore feet, and a bad skin rash.

Day 47: Zamora to
El Cubo de Tierra del Vino – 35 km

Shut the door behind me feeling very lonely. Crossed the stone bridge over the River Duero leaving Zamora and Tammy behind.

Must have taken a wrong road, came to a junction not on the map I had sketched. Noticed the autovía ahead, knew I was not where I ought to be, could not walk on the hard shoulder. Bordering the length of the autovía I observed a few feet of earth works sloping down to a ditch. Decided to walk along this, only the safety barrier between myself and traffic. A few more kilometres to the junction should get me right back on course. The pressure on my ankles from traversing the incline proved too much, so I descended into the filthy ditch half full with greyish liquid and floating debris. Walking on the dirty silt I knew my feet could be washed, but my ankles could not be risked. Not the best way to start the day, it was either the silty broth or a long march back to correct my error.

On my own again, left to my own devices, I had strayed from the path – oh how I missed Tammy!

Reached Morales del Vino, bought some stuff and fruit, yes fruit, had breakfast. On to Corrales del Vino; what, more wine? A few kilometres on passed the little village of Peleas de Arriba and into a lovely wooded area, Valparaiso.

On the other side of the road by the woods was a young couple. They were filling up dozens of 5 litre bottles from a fountain in a hollowed out recess. I approached and they encouraged me to drink and refill my own bottles. They told me that this water had medicinal properties, that many come to this fountain in the hope its healing powers can alleviate their ailments.

Very hot, lucky there was shade! A placard on the side of the road explained the history of the area. The region had first been cultivated by monks who built a monastery in the woods. The King had visited and a chapel erected to commemorate the event.

Got to my destination, El Cubo de Tierra del Vino. In for a good night sleep in a bucket of wine!

Opted for one of two albergues in town. María, my hostess told me it was 8 € for a bed in a shared room of four, or double that for your own room with shared bathroom. A no-brainer, did not want to put up with three snoring pilgrims!

I have slept in many albergues over the years and through my many Caminos. Imagine lying on a creaking bunk-bed, maybe dozens of bunks close on either side. A large room filled with fifty pilgrims, or more! Lights out at 2200 hrs, then curtains up for the opera. Snoring, coughing, farting, moving around, getting up, shuffling feet, and sometimes even singing! You get up to go and there is someone using the toilet. Five in the morning alarms ring and pilgrims shuffling around packing their kit and shining torchlight on your face.

Would avoid shared quarters at all cost during the Walk to the Rock, that sort of night life might be acceptable for a week or two but not for 75 days. Proper rest was vital, the same applied to other pivotal requirements like water, light-weight kit, nourishment, and my sandals. My feet would have not carried me for so long in boots.

Shared my supper with three pilgrims. Joaquín from Madrid, who had been living in Cádiz for the last twenty-five years. He started in Seville, this his first walk. Joaquín, a lawyer, had done his National Service as a gunner posted in La Línea de la Concepción (border town with Gibraltar), in the 70's, retiring as a Colonel. Eva, a Dutch mid-wife seeking change and carrying far too much, including a dictionary and heavy Camino guide-book. This was her second day, starting in Salamanca. Juliano, Italian but born in Liege, Belgium, identified with Italy in Belgium and felt Belgian when visiting Italy. He carried little weight, and also begun in Seville. María served a generous slap-up home-made meal which we devoured whilst the jugs of wine kept coming, after all, it was all about the vino around here!

Day 48: El Cubo de Tierra del Vino
to Salamanca – 38 km

Up early, on the Nacional 630 all day, a tedious long walk on sticky tarmac. Couldn't find a place to stop and eat till 20 km in, eventually sat for a hearty breakfast and long rest. The bar filled up with locals, here for their morning dose of alcohol to see them through the day. Spent an hour contemplating the passage of time and eavesdropping on conversations.

Whenever I stop I make it a habit to take off my sandals. Many pilgrims keep their boots on when at rest, this is lazy behaviour. It is absolutely necessary to take care of your feet, rub ointment, massage, change socks or refresh in cool water. Two pilgrims at the table next to me said hello, I ordered café con leche, NATO standard.*

The road ahead cut through flat cultivated land and disappeared into the distance, emerging further on. Trudged on reaching the edge of Salamanca. Took some time to get to the centre through busy roads.

Salamanca is always a good stop. A university city brimming with street life, arts and culture, attractive architecture, and perhaps the best Plaza Mayor in all of Spain. This was my third time in the city. In 2010 Tammy's bicycle gave up the ghost 30 km from Salamanca. Masking tape and a bit of luck saved the day. Bought a new bicycle matching her red cycling top.

Found a cheap hostel overlooking la Plaza Mayor, during the evening it got progressively rowdier but it didn't bother me. Went for a walk along medieval streets and found a place to sit down for a robust glass of red. Ambled along adjacent roads and plazas, Saturday evening and the eateries were chock a bloc. Had to sit inside.

Asked for a selection of 10 tapas for 10 €, could not believe the quantity and variety! An American tourist inquired on whether he should order the same, I replied "only if you have a big appetite". He wiped his plate clean, I conceded well before desert!

These past six days have been tough. Following la Vía de la Plata in the opposite direction is not easy, nor are tarmac roads. Being with Tammy was the highlight of the week.

As I head south it is getting hotter. Have to start earlier to beat the midday sun, carrying much more water, my pack considerably heavier – my effort all the greater.

*Coffee, white, two sugars.

Day 49: Salamanca to La Maja – 37 km

Walked out of Salamanca in the dark, crossed the Roman bridge at 0500 hrs. Had been warned of complications exiting the city on the Nacional 630 due to traffic. My early start eliminated that concern. Bought a new road map as my route diverges from la Vía de la Plata for the next few days.

Roads and more roads. Slowed my pace today, took it easy. Not an enjoyable trail, the temperatures rose, my hike progressively harsher. Did not see a single soul, could hear crickets chirp chirping merrily away. A monotonous day.

Saw a variety of tarmacs of different grain and shades and considered compiling an index for future reference, classifying the grade, thickness, and colour. Sun beat down, started singing and slow marched to La Maja. What a horrible day, so different to the pilgrim filled tracks of the north.

Showering wearing sandals was the most exciting thing I did today, maybe that was for the best. In 2013 I was walking the Camino del Norte with Carl, an elderly Swiss gentleman. He told me that on his first Camino he trod on a bar of soap in the shower and awoke naked on the floor in a pool of his own blood. He had a broken arm, cracked ribs, fractured hip, and severe concussion. Carl had to be medevacked back to Switzerland, returning to complete the French Way after a full recovery. I thought, well maybe, just maybe, a little boredom ain't so bad.

Day 50: La Maja to Béjar – 41 km

Started early, feeling frisky and fleet of foot. Had a few short breaks and got to Guijuelo in good time. This area is known for quality jamón serrano, cured Spanish ham. Pressed on and got up Puerto Vallejera at 1200 m. Cooler now, more like my kind of walking weather. The terrain changed considerably, I left the flat open ground and entered the mountains.

Felt the Camino was turning against me. It became a battle of wills, of road versus sandals. Very bored, very alone. This led to doubt and indecision. Maybe I could find a nice secluded bodega by the road and hole up for a couple of days, weeks even... had to maintain my focus – complete my mission – Walk to the Rock!

Singing Beatles tracks did the trick. I never wear earphones while walking, any audio can be very dangerous. Covering one of the five senses is potentially a fatal distraction on the road.

Trees towered over the desolate road providing a canopy against the unyielding sun. Reached the summit, an immense feeling of joy and pride. My heart beat hard in my chest, well aware of the effort. Sharp short breathes were all I was able to command at this point. The hardest stretch was over and done with.

Found a comfortable spot in the shade of a large oak and unwrapped my bocadillo of the day, lifting it to my mouth. A bee zeroed in, buzzing noisily around my head. Swatted it, felt a sharp prick on the back of my hand. Ouch! Bit and sucked at the stinger. Returning to my lunch I couldn't help but remember a chance encounter with a Polish pilgrim during my first Camino, way back in 2009.

That year, whilst resting on the steps of a cruceiro, a stone cross, in the middle of the vast meseta of Castilla y León, a Polish pilgrim had sat beside me and partook in a shared lunch. He had recently been discharged from hospital after ten days recovering from a bee sting! Jan was outside a bar having a drink when, raising the glass to his mouth, a truly vicious bee stabbed the flesh of his tongue. Unable to articulate a call for help, Jan found his throat swollen shut, gagging for air he collapsed.

The next thing Jan recalls is waking in the back of an ambulance with a respirator tied to his face. He had suffered an intense allergic reaction resulting in shock and a mild seizure. Lucky, he said, that a good Samaritan acted quick and kept him alive till the medics arrived. After being released from hospital Jan went on to complete his Camino. Thankfully, my hand was only a little worse for wear!

Stopped at Béjar, a quaint town. Uphill is infinitely preferable to the boring plains, more of it tomorrow, good.

Day 51: Béjar to Plasencia – 57 km

Followed the Nacional 630 road out of town, roughly 5 km on to Cantagallos, 4 km more to Puerto de Béjar. All up hill, was enjoying the winding road up the mountain pass. Started very early, decided to get to the top before halting for a spot of breakfast.

The road led into Extremadura, left Castilla y León behind. The Roman calzada is the best preserved I had ever seen. Followed it all the way down to los Baños de Montemayor. If the Romans travelled these roads all over their extensive empire wearing only sandals (and without sunglasses!) I could do the same.

In 2010 Tammy and I stopped here on our bicycles. On the upper area of the town was a large natural recess fed by a pipe of cool mountain water. We swam and basked in the sun. Los Baños de Montemayor is well known as a health spa, many come from afar for the healing effects of its waters. This time around I was disappointed to find it empty, no frolicking today.

That night in 2010 we slept in an empty albergue, no one to greet us on our arrival. We simply followed written instructions left by the entrance and I put some money into a collection box.

Could see a lake and towns on the horizon, mountains and more mountains and blue skies. Left the Nacional 630 diverging onto a side track only to be confronted by a herd of goats.

At Aldeanueva del Camino I sat down for a second breakfast and had a conversation with two road sweepers. One of them had been raised in Australia and later lived in London. "There is nothing for the youth around here" he said. "Twenty left for London last week in search of work". This was a recurring fact everywhere I went.

The conversation turned to Gibraltar, and Miguel asked "shouldn't Gibraltar be given back to Spain?" I responded "what about Ceuta and Melilla?"

Miguel smiled, "touché". Conversed at length about corruption in Spain, the monarchy, unemployment, and how Gibraltar remained an issue of national pride for many Spaniards.

"Miguel," I said, "Gibraltar employs over 6000 Spanish workers. We are the most stable financial influence to the Campo area. With a distinct culture, we are a tolerant and charitable society. And you know what has forged us into what we are – British Gibraltarian? Spain! Your persistence to recover what you lost in battle 311 years ago!"

Aldeanueva survives on agriculture, chiefly the production of pimentón – paprika. Miguel told me he missed Australia and wished he had remained in London.

Made good time, wasn't too hot. Two hours later got to a hostel, my intended stop for the day. Went in, re-hydrated, and ate the compulsory slice of potato tortilla after which I got a nervous tickle in my stomach, that feeling that launches me into other possibilities. What the heck, I was here to walk, sunset was still pretty far off!

A fresh wind at my back. Was getting cooler and I had been going for hours when I heard a distinctive peal of thunder, rain followed shortly. What a welcome change! Pushed on from Jarilla, another 23 km to Plasencia through winding roads and over Monte Valcorchero. 3 peaches, a banana, 2 litres of water, and 4 cereal bars got me to the entrance of town. I moved through the centre – it was feria time. Noticed a large area where the fair had been set up and many people milling around. Seriously considered having a go on the biggest bouncy castle I had ever seen.

Would I break the 60 km barrier? Nearly, but not quite. The weather behaved well, felt quite strong at the moment and was willing to risk. No longer afraid of failure, my fears had given way to a certainty – I would make it! Feet are fine, just a bit sore. No muscle ache and only a slight headache, but I get those everyday, walk or not – from my cranky neck and lower back problems.

Day 52: Plasencia to Cañaveral – 42 km

Left Plasencia feeling apprehensive as the Placentinos were in full fiesta swing. Walking on the Nacional 630, across the River Jerte and uphill. Following the road all day is boring, however, most Caminos are only yards away from a road. Encountered some traffic initially but mostly had the road to myself. At Grimaldo saw a castle similar to the Tower of Homage in Gibraltar, had to approach to make sure it wasn't inflatable!

I had a flat tire somewhere around here, cycling in 2010. Tammy assisted changing the inner tube when a Guardia Civil patrol car pulled up and the officers offered to help. "No need," I said. They wished us a buen camino and went on their way. Things hadn't changed much since then, only now I was going downhill, an easy final 7 km.

Cañaveral, had a beer and settled down. After yesterday's brutal distance, worried that I wouldn't be able to keep up the pace.

Completely focused on target and destination, no concerns for time. Accustomed now to the routine, my eating habits modified to take little nourishment. I am expending an enormous amount of energy, burning calories at a very fast rate. Feel trimmer, more compact, have lost substantial flab.

Day 53: Cañaveral to Cáceres – 39 km

Took the Nacional 630 out of town parallel to the Embalse de Alcántara, a large reservoir fed by the Río Tajo. The Camino diverges considerably here and follows the high ground. Crossed a bridge or two and continued to border the embalse. Rested at La Perala, another stop at the polígono industrial* of Casar de Cáceres. They make nice cheese here, Tortas de Casar. Entering Cáceres with heavy traffic on a Friday afternoon was not pleasant.

Late afternoon, deep in slumber when the call came through on my tablet. "Have I woken you up?" Replied "yeah, thanks mum no worries, great timing". Ended the call, back to some shut eye. Ring, ring; "hi darling (the wife), have I woken you?" I said "you can wake me up whenever you wish."

*Industrial estate.

"Remember now," Michelle said, "leave some talking for tomorrow when you meet James!"

His train got in at 2145 hrs. Glad to see James Gracia, the newly appointed Regimental Second in Command (2IC). He'd given up a long weekend to join me on the Camino. We spoke about the coming days and old times over a good bottle of local tinto.

This had been the longest phase in the shortest time. A combination of good physical condition, cool weather, and wanting to reach Cáceres in time to meet James drove me to attain 216 km in just five days. Now feel the worst is over. Could afford to walk shorter distances as I head into the south summer heat.

Day 54: Cáceres to Cruce de Las Herrerias – 37 km

Up at 0545 hrs, slick routine, on the road by 0620 hrs. In half an hour we were at the periphery of the city on the Nacional 630. James saw how difficult it was to follow the Camino in reverse. He wore heavy boots and I feared for his feet.

At 0750 hrs we passed a military barracks with no sign of life, laughed our heads off when ten minutes later we heard reveille played over loud speakers. What! "Late start or time for churros and coffee?"

James – leaving Cáceres in the dark

14 km from the start we knew there was a bar at Valdesalor. Halted for a good rest and substantial breakfast – tostatadas con jamón y tomate, and home-made pastries. The roads were chock full of cars coming off the autovía stopping for a bite.

We continued, talking and walking, "well," James remarked; "you talked, I walked!" Deep in conversation when an approaching vehicle cut over the white line, straight at us, swerving back out at the last moment. He rolled down his window waving his hands, shouting incomprehensibly, making the point that the road was his.

We shook our poles hoping he would pull over and get thumped in the face. Two or three Guardia Civil vehicles passed us today. All slowed down, pulled away from us and waved as they passed.

Proceeded on the Camino as it ran parallel to the road. Came across a couple of pilgrims heading in the correct direction, towards Santiago. Overcast skies and a fresh wind made our walk a lot easier. El Cruce de Las Herrerias in time for a late lunch and settled down for the day. Showered, with clothes on (!), had a good long siesta. Went down for a bottle of red or two, and of course, lots more talk!

We reminisced about a hike in Wales way back when I had been the 2IC, the post James held now. In 2002, during the R&R phase (a few days off), of a battalion camp in Sennybridge we got together to do a little hill walking.

The plan was to go up the Pen y Fan, the highest peak in the Brecon Beacons Natural Park. Right next door is Corn Du, the second highest peak. Pen y Fan and Corn Du together are known as Arthur's Seat. We wanted to go up both. Two of our lads were setting off on a harder trek to test themselves, one of them was preparing for selection. This area is used by the UK Special Forces for their selection process, so it was a good idea to familiarize with the ground. As recently as 2013 three soldiers have died attempting selection, collapsing of exhaustion during Exercise Fan Dance.

James and I surmounted both peaks, descending to an attractive body of water. When we got to the reservoir realised that we had travelled out of the edge of our map and were far from the pre-arranged pick up point.

Carried away by our passion, things had gone pear shaped! Military instinct and guess work took over, it was getting dark now, wait, what's that? Hark, a single spark of light in the cold and dark, a solution to all our ills – a pub!

After our second pint I took it upon myself to call barracks and arrange for a pick up. Unable to communicate directly with Camp we had to call Gibraltar, the Adjutant Captain Andrew Bonfante answered.

"Lost? Are you lost Mark?" Andrew asked.

"Well...err, not really, jut not exactly where we intended to be..." I replied.

"Understood! I shall organise a rescue mission for you, Sir!" I heard giggling as he put down the phone.

40 minutes later, the Commanding Officer Francis Brancato strolled into the pub, behind him the rescue team; the RSM WO1* Eddie Asquez grinning from ear to ear. Eddie saluted saying, "get the pints in, Sir!"

Lesson learnt – we all lose our way from time to time, but if you intend to take refuge in a pub make sure that the RSM is not part of the rescue team!

Day 55: Cruce de Las Herrerias to Mérida – 35 km

Ate too much, our supper was late and consisted of delicious greasy Iberian pork. Slept well, in the morning we both felt bloated. On the road by 0600 hrs walking in the dark, wanted to get to Mérida early so that James could see the sights. Chewed the fat for hours, having a companion made a world of difference.

The only town on our route was Aljucén, some 18 km away. Early on a Sunday, not a single open bar or shop. James was beginning to come to terms to life without coffee. Short break, rifled through emergency rations and continued on. Started to pour. Weather was cool, cloudy, excellent for walking. By 1315 hrs we were in Mérida.

Founded in 23 BC as a settlement for veterans of the Iberian wars, Mérida contains more important remains of Roman antiquity than any other town in Spain. It boasts an

*Regimental Sergeant Major, Warrant Officer Class 1.

amphitheatre, which is still used, an ancient stone bridge over the River Guadiana, the National Museum of Roman Art, Trajan's Arch and more. We spent the afternoon breathing history. What a fantastic place, well worth a visit!

On another occasion, caravanning with Michelle, I had sampled Mérida's bacalao dorado for the first time. Ordered a dish of bacalao (cod), scrambled eggs, and potato sticks for us now. James asked for seconds, and more of same the next day!

Gabbed about everything under the sun. James told me about his plan to visit Everest Base Camp, and the conversation turned to the dangers of mountains, disasters, and avalanches. Both of us remembered how in Sierra Nevada, near Granada, Spain, in 1992 Captain Frank Galliano lost his life in a tragic skiing accident. Others came close to death that day. One of these was Gerard Fitzgerald, recently retired Regimental Second in Command.

Together with Ivor Lopez and Ronnie Wallace we had walked to the area, Gerard identified the spot of the accident and we placed the commemorative plaque in memory of Frank. I have been there on numerous occasions, every two years more or less. Last year James, Tammy, and Dan Mifsud had gone up to the valley and visited the plaque.

Day 56: Mérida to Almendralejo – 34 km

Crossed the long bridge out of Mérida, onto the road with heavy traffic coming into the city. James insisted on a quick coffee at the last bar out of town. The Camino was in a bad state from the rain of the previous day.

Saw four pilgrims today. One of them, a Spanish lady who stopped and asked whether she was going the right way. James was alarmed by the state of her rucksack, her clothing and a bag of food hung on the outside. A second smaller bag around her neck, and a very large sleeping bag at her rear knocking against her legs. She said "Santiago?" Replied pointing behind us "si, Santiago that a-ways."

It was her first day!

Explained to James how little many pilgrims knew about walking, how ill-prepared and badly equipped they were. I had, over numerous years, met pilgrims that were not deterred by abysmal kit.

James had seen the sandal-light and converted. He shed his boots, which over the last two days gave him several blisters, and now walked in my spare sandals.

This morning I woke with a sore throat, temperature, stuffy nose, and light of head. Informed James that most likely I wouldn't be having any alcohol today. He did not hesitate to illuminate the medicinal properties of wine. Truly impressive powers of persuasion, took him thirty seconds to convince me! A good bottle of red cures any ailment, if consumed regularly. The walk today was all roads.

Almendralejo, had a good lunch with a smooth but spicy red cough syrup. James departs tomorrow. I continue my journey south, now about 200 km from Seville.

Dr James and his medicinal spicy red cough syrup

Day 57: Almendralejo to Zafra – 36 km

Body clock got me up at 0500 hrs, James did not depart till 0815 hrs. Had planned to sleep in and leave with him. Instead, I said my farewells and was out by 0600 hrs. We are good in the military at keeping strict habits. It requires discipline, particularly when involved in projects of prolonged duration.

Soldiers on operational tours are adept at maintaining standards day in, day out. On their return it may be difficult to adjust to a normal routine, I have experienced this multiple times.

James must have taken all the good walking weather. The merciful cloud cover and refreshing breeze of the weekend were gone. By 0900 hrs the sun was slow cooking the left side of my face. Took precautions, applying sun cream and wetting my head, frequently taking cover in the shade. Suffered a terrible headache all day, drank plenty and applied a copious amount of Tiger Balm to my head and eyes.

The traffic was incessant. Continued to walk the Nacional 630, the main motorway close by. Asked a passer-by why it was so busy, all I got was; "it shouldn't be!" Left the Nacional 630 and took another road towards Los Santos de Maimona. At the end of a park saw an underground walkway for pedestrians. Took refuge from the sun and lay there for a long time.

No one came into the tunnel. Many memories of similar dark and dingy places came to mind. I have spent up to a week on exercise living inside Gibraltar's extensive tunnel system. There are over 55 km of passage ways hewn inside the Rock, waking up in darkness it is impossible to tell night from day! Picked myself up and slogged on – no rest for the wicked.

Day 58: Zafra to Fuente de Cantos – 28 km

Last night I contemplated staying in Zafra an extra day. Previous rest day had been on June 01st with Tammy in Astorga. Woke up early, loo, brush teeth, pack kit, prepare feet, check under the bed, out of the door. No rest day today, my body was ready to keep moving. Pharmacy thermometer flashed 18°c at 0630 hrs.

The Nacional 432 out of Zafra, unnervingly busy both ways. Two hours to get to the junction with the Nacional 630, some 6.5 km. Overtaking, using mobile phones, smoking, speeding, less than a metre apart! Had to leave the road often to avoid injury, a nightmare of honking horns and tires spitting gravel into my face.

The closest town was Calzadilla de los Barros, 19 km. Nothing between here and there, all I had was a Kit Kat and some mini Oreos. At one point I found the Camino and followed it. By 1000 hrs the sun beat down from windless blue skies. Passed sunflower fields, olive trees, and budding vines. Had to wet my head and neck constantly, didn't want another headache. Energy reserves went right down. Had to stop, to eat, to rest, to get to the town. Maybe I should have taken that rest day after all.

A deep crack developed on the hard skin of my right heel, more painful with every step. Knew that with the right care and treatment it would heal. All I could do for now was keep on walking, applying antiseptic cream, and grit my teeth. It would get better.

Arrived at Calzadilla de los Barros, ate some fruit, a big bocadillo, some sugary stuff, and plenty of drink. Temperature over 30°C, another 7 km to end the day. Refreshed, pushed hard and covered the distance in an hour and a half.

I could afford to slow down, cover 20/25 km a day and still be home by 04th July, finishing before the sun is at its worst. Must keep in mind though, distance is dictated by available accommodation, am not equipped to rough it.

Day 59: Fuente de Cantos to Monesterio – 29 km

On the road very early admiring a stunning skyline over flat fields. Hoofed it out of Fuente de Cantos past various mataderos, slaughter-houses. A putrid odour lingered in the warm morning air. 5 km on there was a petrol station. A pack of sandwiches, crisps, Kit Kat, and exorbitant vending machine coffee was the best I could do for my first meal of the day. Pilgrims can't be choosers, could have murdered a good fry-up!

Next section of road was different, entertaining – it had bends and considerably more hills. Something to break up the monotony. Hundreds of beer bottles lay smashed by the side of the road where a lorry had no doubt shed its cargo. Lost count after 22 green bottles! Surroundings were evolving, I knew that tomorrow I would cross over to Andalucía. Soldiered on, was only 0800 hrs but felt like tea time!

Dammed hot. Kept pushing the jelly uphill to Monesterio. A supermarket, civilization at last! Too early to call it a day, the crack on my right heel less painful. Ate something and decided to go on. Passed pilgrims struggling uphill as I limbered down a very steep descent.

Poor fellows, they were sweating buckets. A little later got to my destination; service station 8 km past Monesterio on the Nacional 630. Now less than 100 km to Seville.

Day 60: Monesterio to Almadén de la Plata – 32 km

Walked on tracks and minor roads following la Vía de la Plata from Real de la Jarra to Almadén de la Plata. Spied two castles and another at a distance, Santa Olalla – had been there with Michelle on a caravan road trip. There are hundreds of castles and stone forts in this region dating back to the times of the Reconquista.[*]

Passed extensive pasture land – dehesas, the favoured grazing ground for cerdos ibericos, Iberian pigs. They roamed about, feeding and rolling in dirt. Huge beasts being fattened for the plate, couldn't but feel sorry that they weren't already cured and hanging from the shop window! They looked tasty even on four legs.

The deep crack on my right heel healed, no more agony. By 0900 hrs it was already boiling. Crossed over into Andalucía, heat forced me to seek refuge in the shade of an old oak. Ants were having a feast with my left over lunch. Had been pushing too hard, far too hot now to maintain this daily pace. Very concerned about wear and tear. The accumulation of walking weeks sapping my strength, felt exhausted down to my bones.

Over the next bend a view opened up and I never before thought that such splendour could hurt my eyes. Sloping hills held a forest of cork trees, cattle grazing, the swooping and shrieks of birds, and constant buzz of crickets from every bush.

A sudden passion filled my body. I lost myself in day dreams, my wife, wished she could be here, could see what I saw, feel what I felt. Not sad, not quite happy, a strange in-between. Elation and longing, a joyful torment knowing I loved and was loved, but am at this moment alone.

Days end, shower, tend to feet, wash shirt and underpants. Time for rest and drink, eat, and write. Everyday I'm writing now, keeping a record best I can. In the evening I hardly eat, look ahead to the next day and prepare.

*Reconquest of the Iberian Peninsula from the Islamic Caliphates by the Christians between the 700's and 1400's.

Day 61: Almadén to Castilblanco – 33 km

Over 30 km on minor roads today, did not want to be caught out in the open at the sun's zenith. Weather forecast warned of extreme high temperatures – alerta roja, red alert. Walked very fast in the pre dawn, flashing headlamp warned of my presence. Surprised at the number of Land Rovers from the Departamento de Agricultura which sped by.

The first few kilometres were uphill, getting warm already. The road alternated up and down and around many bends. A car pulled over, a young man offering a lift. I refused and thanked him, continued uphill for 3 or 4 km.

0900 hrs, stopped, drank about half a litre of water, had some bread, cheese, and smoked pork. Already walked a fair distance. A few kilometres on saw a pilgrim, then another two. Bid them buen camino. They crossed the road, asked about the route ahead, and whether I'd been to Santiago.

Really nice fellows, and like most Italians I have met, very outgoing. Reminded me of my friend Erasmo from the Camino Francés a few years ago. Tammy and I walked with him in 2013 for a few days and got to know him well.

That year, Erasmo and Mike (the Texan) had met up with us in Astorga just after our 50 km hike. These guys could really shift! On their final approach to Santiago they force-marched close to 70 km, nearly being arrested when arriving at cathedral square at two in the morning!

Onwards and upwards, ultreia!* Got harder and dammed hot. My feet were dry, sore, searched for a stream but was out of luck. Paused regularly to down a few gulps of water and wet my hair and head. Was ready for this type of heat;

*Camino greeting meaning onwards and upwards, often used in the past.

not been a problem in so far as I started early and was able to cover the distances in good time.

1300 hrs, arrived at Castilblanco de los Arroyos. Found a room in a hostel for 12 €, shared toilet though, but no one else came. Ate at a small place with great food. Got chatty with two retired couples. We laughed and joked about Gibraltar and Spain, discussed the days of empire, the Armada, and the surrounding towns. Fernando, a retired doctor now dedicated to karate, was on his way to Bratislava for a competition.

Temperatures soared to 35°C.

Day 62: Castilblanco to Seville – 41 km

There was a fiesta at the big hotel exiting town. Warned to be careful on my way out. Left early, 0600 hrs, negotiating through streets thick with youth. Endured booming music from passing cars instead of the normal dawn silence. They were very loud, but driving responsibly, some shouted and hooted. I was pleasantly surprised by their attitude, my prejudices entirely shattered.

Moving downhill over a rocky section I came to a spaghetti junction with numerous diverging tracks. Ok, which way Mark? There were bicycle tracks, yellow arrows, red and white markings, all pointing away from the intersection. Not much use.

Flipping a coin in my head I decided on the right-hand route. After a few minutes, still couldn't find signs. Turned around and went back, took the next track. Fifty metres on was a yellow arrow on a rock, success! Sometimes you have to go back to go forward, obvious as it seems.

Lovely countryside, very similar to walking in the Campo de Gibraltar.* My first view of Seville on the horizon. Intention was to get to Santiponce, near the ruins of the Roman city of Italica, and tomorrow walk through Camas and into Seville.

Through an orange grove, met my only pilgrim of the day. He was wearing headphones and passed straight by without a second glance. 2 km further to Guillena, was 0930 hrs, had walked 19 km. Breakfast, the usual toast with garlic, olive oil and tomato set me right for the next stage to Santiponce. A call from Michelle, said I was fine and would get to Seville tomorrow. Undulating countryside, ups and downs and ups again, but I could relax and enjoy the walking – time was now on my side.

No plan survives initial contact with the enemy – the foe here being my sense of direction! 2 km from town, no markers, crippling heat, a fork in the road. Oh no! Time for that coin flip again, eh? Tails; left it is. Looking good, looking good – continued along the path at a brisk pace. Both routes seemed to be going in the general direction of Santiponce, so the assumption was that I'd get there one way or another.

Said it before, finding the marked Camino in reverse is a nightmare! This is not like the French Way where pilgrims are thick as flies. Today I decided that it would be alright to go a little off-road as I was near to Seville and wanted to avoid traffic. My first mistake, a sharp reminder of why I walked the Nacional 630 for most of the way. Guess I grew a little complacent closer to home.

Somehow, don't ask me how, found myself on the wrong side of la Rivera de Huelva. Not where I was supposed to be at all. Travailing the beautiful river bank rich with wildlife, came upon a field with dozens of boxes which, by the buzz, I

*Spanish name for the area around Gibraltar.

118

deduced were bee hives. Hesitated, recalled Jan – did not want to end my Camino victim to killer bees! Took the plunge, passed rapidly a few yards from a swarm. Phew! Nerve-racking as it was, they didn't even notice I existed.

Now accepted I would not be passing Santiponce. Found an alternative path that led to the town of La Algaba, not far from Seville. Came across a herd of goats and stopped to talk with the cabrero, a goatherd. Antonio tended the herd for pleasure as a favour to his son-in-law, enjoying being outdoors. His two dogs barked at me, good dogs! Doing their job protecting the goats. They reminded me of Poppy, my deceased mutt who'd been a loyal companion for over seventeen years.

There was an incident, years ago now, when Poppy came running up to me, her mouth and face covered in blood! At the time we lived in a house with a big garden at Europa Flats, near the mosque at Europa Point – the south-most tip of Gibraltar. We looked in the garden and saw that one of our two pet ducks was missing. Hmm. Evidence was strong against the poor mutt. Poppy could not escape a stern talking to! The kids cried for Quacky, scolding the sorry pooch.

Days later we woke to loud quacking, rushed out and saw Quacky emerge from the cactus bushes! An inspection of the garden revealed a rat, dead in the thicket. Poppy had done her duty – protecting her duck brother. We were all very apologetic and she was rewarded with double rations for the next few weeks.

Antonio offered a cigarette, pointing the way for me, more or less. Got to Torre de la Reina and followed a polígono industrial, round a roundabout and on to La Algaba. That day I got to Seville.

Antonio el cabrero, his dogs reminded me of Poppy

Day 63: Sevilla

Did not wake at the crack of dawn, lazed around in bed for a few more hours. Rest day today, the first in 730 km!

Planned to leave Seville tomorrow. Would be two to three hundred kilometres to Gibraltar, depending on which way I decided to go once past Jerez de la Frontera. I fully intended to cross the border on 04th July; the 100th anniversary of the formation of the Gibraltar Volunteer Corps in 1915. That was my plan, my singular determination, and I was certain I would make it.

Met Francisco, a coachman who became a friend in 2010. Went for a few beers and tapas. Francisco is an aficionado to la Vía de la Plata on horseback, so we had a few things in common!

7

Sevilla to Gibraltar

"The Mountain of Tarik is like a beacon spreading its rays over the sea, rising far above the neighbouring mountains. One might fancy that its face almost reaches the sky and that its eyes are watching the stars in the celestial track."

~8th century Moorish poet~

Day 64: Sevilla to Utrera – 39 km

0400 hrs, made my way through the streets of Seville. An early start as the city is well lit and this time I made sure to have my city map handy. Would take time to clear the urban area, traffic lights, major crossing points, and lots of cars. Under a road, across a junction, this was dragging on and the city was waking up, traffic building. Followed a minor street into Dos Hermanas, a largish town close to Seville, now 0815 hrs. Sat down for a little breakfast.

Asked a taxi driver for directions, they can always be trusted to give good information. Dos Hermanas is a large town and didn't want to spend more time than necessary navigating it. Over the railway line, roughly 3 km to the outskirts of town, and through a permanent fair ground. A further 7 km by the railway track; people had been using the path as a dump. Human waste, debris, bits of tiles, and split bin bags. Had to use my walking poles to keep the flies off my face, this went on for a good few kilometres. Was not pleasant. Numerous trains sped by in both directions.

The path led over the railway onto a lovely country lane. Shaded olive groves on both sides, rabbits running in and out of holes. Noticed an area rich with prickly pears and a straw

121

hatted fellow using a long pole to collect them with great ease. Asked how he rid the prickly pears of their spines; I'd seen this done using a broom, sweeping the fruit across sandy ground.

The man explained his method was to put the prickly pears in a bucket of water, let them stand, using a net shaped as a funnel, empty the pears into the river. After a few minutes they'd emerge clean and spineless!

In Utrera I got a call from Steve Brown, ex Gibraltar Regiment soldier with a show on Drystone Radio in the UK. Went live on air, questioned on the walk, distances, weather, my motivations, and the charity. Steve understood military mentality – once a soldier always a soldier!

Day 65: Utrera to Lebrija – 53 km

Not slept well, 21st June, Midsummer Night. In Spain this is a Christian festival, La Vispera or Noche de San Juan, St John the Baptist. Bonfires blazed in the street below my window. In the hotel bar an all night disco thumped out bass heavy tunes. Did not get much shut eye. During a previous Camino in 2012 I spent a delightful Noche de San Juan around a bonfire drinking beer with pilgrims. On that occasion I had embraced the celebration, there had been a B-B-Q serving potatoes, sausages, steak, and hot coals laid out for the foolhardy to walk gingerly over.

Walked 15 km on road, a tiring slog on hot tarmac. Picked up the trail across a railway line and under the motorway. Stopped for a break, two tatty arm chairs, a defaced half burned doll, the remains of a simmering tire, and a starving dog with eyes the size of saucers. Could've believed I was walking through a BBC docudrama on poverty in the Third World. Sat by some rocks and had some food, dog kept its distance. Chucked a scrap of jamón serrano which was swiftly devoured.

Speeding cars and trucks echoed above on the road. Who would sit on an arm chair under the motorway and burn a doll? I had seen similar dolls in other places, tied to fences outside derelict buildings, and around polígonos industriales. Some defaced, others dressed, burnt, a noose round their neck, nails and sharp items stuck in them. Some type of paganism? Witchcraft? Maybe just boredom, heck if I know.

As for the stray mutt, don't think it was there for any ritual. Came back but kept a distance, chucked it half a muffin. Found a plastic container from the rubbish, poured some water. The dog ate the stale bread drunk from the bowl.

Followed the Canal Bajo del Guadalquivir. On both sides there was agricultural land extending as far as the eye could see. Passed fields of corn, of tomatoes, cotton, sunflowers, lettuce and groves of olive trees.

A gentleman with a wide brimmed straw hat tended to a corn field. He got up, smiled and said "buenos días". Inquired on the route ahead, he gave directions and asked about my walk. Juan told me there were another 15 km to Las Cabezas de San Juan. His nephew, he said, is studying in Algeciras, and Juan hoped he would come and work with him some day.

Juan was astounded I had walked from Wales. The furthest he'd ever been was a skiing resort north of Madrid, Valdeskqui. He worked there as a crane operator in the 70's, managing to save about 600,000 pesetas, returned home, bought a house, and got married. Once he had taken his wife on holiday all the way to Cádiz! They had no children and he would leave his land to his nephew. Offered to take me to Las Cabezas de San Juan, I politely declined.

Marismilla was in the general direction I would have to take tomorrow. Knew there was accommodation at Las Cabezas de San Juan. Going towards Marismillas would be a risk, but I was here to walk and decided to change the plan, to venture forth.

There was nothing in the town, no albergue, hostel, or hotel. My venturing forth fell flat. Faced with the prospect of humping it back 9 km to Las Cabezas de San Juan, or press on another 18 km. Oh dear oh dear, here we go again, breaking promises. Promised I would walk shorter distances, take it easier. It was 1400 hrs, scorching, and I had already walked 35 km.

Replenished with water and isotonic drink, bought fruit and bread and found a bench in the shade outside a church opposite a bar. A woman passed and gave me the stink eye, I had taken my sandals off and dirty feet were bare to the world. Sweaty, hair and beard unkempt, looking very rugged, more a vagabond than pilgrim!

A breeze picked up, kept me cool – forced myself to stop every 2 km. Tended to my feet, wet my hair. Few cars went by, one stopped and offered a lift, declined. The lift-giver had cycled some of the Camino and understood my wanting to complete on foot. It was blazing, way too hot to be on the road at this time of the day. He said "buen camino!"

Lebrija is a sprawling town which I approached uphill for the last 2 km. Hadn't planned to walk far today, passed the 2000 km barrier.

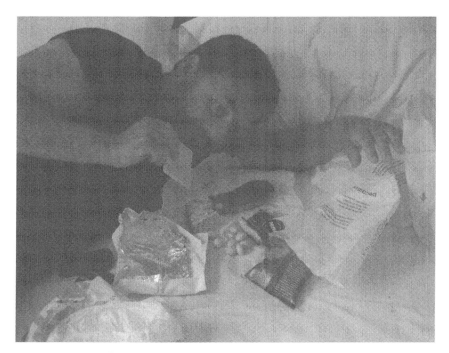

Replenishing lost energy after a tiring day

Day 66: Lebrija to El Cuervo – 11 km

Felt spent after yesterday.

Had a call – the Regiment would be at Casemates, officers on treadmills carrying rucksacks and senior NCO's* would pull a 105 Light Gun. This had all been organized by the RSM WO1 Dean Castrey, informed that they walked 22 km between 0930 and 1330 hrs! What an excellent effort and show of solidarity for my Walk to the Rock.

Shouldn't have walked that much yesterday, concerned about getting to the end too soon! Will have to take more rest days, maybe in Jerez, you know, spend a little time checking out the bodegas.

*Non Commissioned Officers.

Exiting Lebrija I saw a man pushing his car, his pregnant wife behind the wheel. Both of us pushing made the task easier, a hardship shared is a hardship halved after all. Had the car back on the road in no time.

Day 67: El Cuervo to Jerez de la Frontera – 28 km

Dark, only lorry drivers loitering having breakfast at a local café. Flashing head-light announcing my presence to vehicles on la Nacional IV as I departed from El Cuervo. For 4 km followed the busy road, crossed the railway line and onto a small road sign-posted Morabita.

It was around here that in 1972 two trains collided, head-on, resulting in 13 dead. This had been the most serious train accident in Spain up until the crash in Santiago on 24th July 2013. A high speed train derailed, 79 passengers, including some pilgrims, lost their lives. Tammy and I were nearing the end of our walk at the time. We heard the news of the accident and decided it would be best to stay put for a day or two, arrive at Santiago later than the 25th July.

Broken countryside, an exquisite riot of colours. On both sides of the road blooming sunflowers, pale yellow fallow fields dotted with straw bales. Saw rows of viñas which feed the bodegas Jerezanas. Every so often I passed a well kept cortijo, dusty 4x4s and open pens with free running horses.

Left the Nacional IV and approached Jerez on a lonely country road. By 1000 hrs it was the hottest it had been – the heat warning was over 40°c! Managed to shuffle uncomfortably from shade to shade, using up my water reserves very quickly.

Up and down and over hill, stop for cover, drink, rucksack on. Came to a barn which offered welcome shade, stayed for a long time cooling down. Rested, set off in the heat, sweat soon dripping from nose and soaking my shirt.

The lights of Jerez had shone pre dawn from where I'd begun. I rejoiced, over the brow of the next feature saw the city skyline, tall buildings rising from the picturesque rural country. Road sign read; Jerez 2 km. By 1230 hrs reached the centre.

From Seville to Jerez I had experienced extreme temperatures, dusty paths, rugged countryside, and traversed numerous major roads, canals, and railway lines. At Jerez I felt, for the very first time, that I was getting close to the end. Next stage – the final push, the home-run. Took a day of rest, would walk again on Sunday, have to brave the hellish heat and walk!

Day 68: Jerez de la Frontera

Michelle, Matthew and Tammy came to spend two nights. What a difference dinner and conversation with family makes. Felt rejuvenated, the next day visited a bodega sampling several sherries. Heat was suffocating, they could not understand how I could bear walking in these temperatures, and to be frank, neither could I!

Jerez was superb. Hadn't seen Michelle since Santiago, Tammy since Zamora and Matt since I'd left for the UK on 19th April.

Day 69: Jerez to Paterna de Rivera – 38 km

Up at silly hour, set off across the city in the pre-dawn dark. Passed the Monasterio de la Cartuja and Lompardo, made good time to La Ina. Dawn broke, few cars passed by and farmers tended to their fields. Got to a small town, Rajamancera, knew there were 8 km to go to Torrecero.

Somewhere close by is the site of the Battle del Río Guadalete (711/712 AD). Quite where the battle took place is lost to the fog of history. The Moors, under Tarik ibn Ziyad, defeated the Christian Visigoth army of Hispania.

Legend has it that Roderic, the Visigoth king, either died or escaped and hid in a cave and was never seen again. Poof! Gone from history. Hispania lay open to General Tarik. In his honour a remarkable feature was given his name – Jebel Tarik, the Mountain of Tarik – Gibraltar.

It was fiesta time at Torrecero. Found a seat at a table in a place full of people who had been partying all night long. They encouraged me to stay for the bull-run, I declined as there were some 13 km that needed walking. Left at about 1000 hrs, sun unforgiving. The heat warning advised against spending too long in the open, to drink frequently, and to stay in the shade. Didn't have a choice, there was no shade on the road. Wet my head, drank my water, and wore my fancy new straw sombrero. Sure looked cool, but would it be effective? The answer is yes, and very stylish to boot!

1130 hrs, sun was out to defeat me. Honestly felt this was it. A car pulled up and the chap offered a lift, declined. He was baffled, said that what I was doing was dangerous and I could die from "un golpe de calor" – sun stroke. I said I was fine and waved him on.

To my right I could make out Medina-Sidonia, Paterna hidden somewhere ahead. Felt a light breeze on my face and tasted salt. Knew where it came from, filling me with a renewed impetus to go on. Was given wings, glided over the melting tarmac. The scent of home an unexpected pleasure made hardship so much more palatable.

An odd name, I thought, El Perro de Paterna*. Would be lodged there for the night. Paco, the owner, explained that the place was named for his father who had been a renown flamenco singer. Each room named for one of his songs, I was in Granaina.

Freddie Pitto, The Regimental Secretary, had informed me through Facebook about the great food in this area. Absolutely spot on! Right, shall be returning to this one.

Freddie demonstrated support for my adventure from the very beginning, obtaining sponsorship for Walk to the Rock. A journey of this length and duration is obviously quite costly. Thankfully, I had a sterling character like Freddie on my side and half my costs were provided by the Gibunco Group.

That night I shared a bottle of red with locals in la Plaza Mayor of Paterna de Rivera. We spoke about another conflict; the Spanish Civil War. Seven had been shot only yards from where I sipped my wine in la noche de los tiros – 23rd July 1936. Seven others from the town also died that night in a nearby field, shot by the fascists.

Innocent of any crime, it mattered not if they were republicans or communists. Suspected to be anti-facist, they met their fate lined up against the walls of el ayuntamiento. Their accuser; the town priest, a fascist supporter of General Franco. Listened attentively to the horrors they related, how some found refuge in Gibraltar and others went all the way to France.

In 2009 during my first Camino I spent a night at Grañon. Later, I learned the place was sponsored by the Opus Dei, an organisation which some would say has a shady past and supported the Francoist regime. My companions at the time

*The dog of Paterna.

129

dragged me to mass. During the service the priest asked those who spoke Spanish to raise their hands. He asked English speakers, Germans and so on.

My hand went up twice. The priest requested the Spanish to come to the altar and receive a blessing. I remained seated. The priest pointed at me and said, "You there, you raised your hand for Spanish, come forward!" I replied he had said if I spoke Spanish, not if I was Spanish. "Where are you from?" I answered; "Gibraltar!"

"Gibraltar? Gibraltar Español!"

Silence reigned in the House of the Lord as the priest shouted and wagged his finger. My blood boiled, I stood and shouted back at the pulpit; "it is because of fascist priests like you, stuck in the past that I stopped going to church," and stormed out.

What I said in anger is not what I believe to be the truth. Of course not all priests are fascists, I have known some fine priests. My reasons for not attending church were not driven either by fascism or priests. Saying that just felt like the best way of bringing the impertinent holy man down from his dais.

The priest approached me during supper and begun to apologize. He said he had made a mistake and asked for forgiveness. I replied "yes, you have made a mistake and I will not forgive you. You are a priest and should have not mixed politics with religion. You are a fascist, as are those in this country who think Gibraltar theirs. I suggest you go and atone for your sins. Maybe next time you meet a Gibraltarian you'll think twice before you open your mouth." He left con el rabo entre las piernas.[*]

---

*His tail between his legs.

Day 70: Paterna de Rivera to Los Corzos – 19 km

Started a little later, had a shorter distance to trek. Walked for a while heading towards a prominent rock. The sun was shrouded by a veil of cloud, cooler than most mornings.

Asked a local about pit stops and was told there were none. 0915 hrs, very surprised to come across Venta La Liebre, in the middle of nowhere. A lovely coffee and the mother of all toasts with aceite and tomate, all for 2 €!

Don't think I've mentioned the amount of dead creatures I've come across lying on the road while walking the Camino. In this part of Andalucía there were mainly snakes and a few rabbits. In other places I've seen foxes, cats, dogs, rats, hedgehogs, birds and even a cow! Today the roads were carpeted by the corpses of innocent grasshoppers.

Was taken by the scenic landscape, high mountains on the horizon. Cloud had given way to sun, the day heated up as cattle fed by the road and crickets played their repetitious noisy sonata. Following a steep winding descent I got a very clear view of Alcalá de los Gazules and el Picacho and Aljibe, two peaks not far from the town.

Didn't fancy following the long road ascending to town, so took the direct approach up a steep hill right to the top. Found a confitería,* bought a drink and something sweet and the owner followed me outside to smoke a cigarette. Chiri told me that long gone were the days when Alcalá was a compulsory stop for all travellers. Bus loads of people would stop and eat here.

Years ago, returning from a Peninsular Battlefield Tour we stopped in Alcalá for a spot of lunch. Francis and I were tasked with arranging a meal for a large group of Royal

*Confectionery shop.

131

Anglians who had been our hosts. For a thousand of the old pesetas each we had a banquet! Feasted on venison, boar, rabbit, and jugs of sangria. The motorway killed Alcalá. Only now, Chirri said, the local restaurants have begun to resuscitate.

Got to los Corzos; a large service station by the motorway close to Alcalá. My accommodation was at la Palmosa. Waited for my guests for a late lunch. Michelle, Tammy, and my mum Jeanette who I hadn't seen since April. Knew I was in for a hard time! So close to home!

Day 71: Los Corzos to Monte Coche – 28 km

A fine morning for walking. Thick clouds, no sun to be seen, clammy but agreeable. Left los Corzos at 0630 hrs after a spot of brekkie – jumbo toast with zurrapa.* Later reminded of its presence in my belly as I walked a hill!

Hiking on the service road by the autovía, on my left green fields, lightly wooded cotos de caza,+ and lots of cattle. Earlier I was saddened to pass la Venta El Gallo, which I'm sure some of you will recall. Not far from los Corzos on the old Nacional to Jerez it sits, all but abandoned. There is only a large placard up high with the words 'VENTA EL GALLO', another victim of the motorway.

At 1000 hrs the sun broke through the clouds. It became uncomfortably hot, grew desperate for shade. Had to take frequent breaks in the little cover the road provided. Over a tunnel via a service road, through the Benalup roundabout, up the next hill, and over the next tunnel. Tomorrow James

---

*A spread made out of shredded pork and lard, scrumptious!
+Hunting ground or area.

and some of the lads will join me for the walk to Los Barrios, so I wanted to get to a decent start point – Monte Coche.

Found a spot in the shade and lay down for a siesta. Tonight I would sleep in Los Barrios, Michelle picked me up. Stepped through the front door, home but not home. Planned to meet up with the team by the bull ring and drive to the spot I'd stopped today, returning walking.

So very close now, two more walk days, a rest day, and on Saturday 04th July I would enter Gibraltar and do a victory lap around the Rock!

Day 72: Monte Coche to Los Barrios – 30 km

We drove from Los Barrios to Monte Coche at 0630 hrs. Felt fantastic, proud to be accompanied by such a team. Walked at a fast pace, spoke about everything under the sun. James wore his new sandals, using this opportunity to break them in for his coming trek to Everest Base Camp. We were accompanied by Jamie Allen, Company Commander – best job in the world! An extraordinarily fit fellow with many positive ideas for the Regiment. Jose White, Company Second in Command, keen as mustard. Jon Cartwright, part of the old guard, we had been to Canada and Kenya together. Always cheerful, fit, and involved in anything and everything over the years. Alec Spooner, had never met before now, but after only six years in the Regiment he was already with bomb disposal, an all-round adventure type.

Oh how I miss the Regiment!

Monte Coche – Jose, Alec, Jamie, Jon, myself, and James

With weather on our side walking became easy work. Made excellent progress across Monte Coche. This is a beautiful area in the Parque Natural de los Alcornocales, right close to home. I've been here many times walking, cycling, and felt spoilt by magnificent views of the reservoir below. Saw the Rock of Gibraltar, majestic, dominating el Campo area, and across in Africa, Jebel Musa.

Choose a slightly longer track, which I knew to be a nicer walk. We came to the road and on to la Venta El Frenazo. Two rounds of coffee and a little while talking to Kiko, one of three brothers who manage and own the restaurant. He reminded me that if I wished to sell my Volkswagen T3 California he had first refusal! The 'beast' is about twenty-six years old, the last six years together we have struggled up most mountain regions in Spain and Portugal.

Easy going, through orange groves on the Río Palmones. Meandering along for the most part, the walk made short by good company all the way to Los Barrios. A few stiff muscles and sore feet did not deter from going for a slap up lunch and some jars of tinto. Kelly-Anne, from GBC Radio, rang and conducted a brief interview which broadcast the next day.

Day 73: Los Barrios

Woke up in my own bed. My dad, Bob, called and we had a long chat about my travels. Arranged to meet the next day.

Cannot remember that I ever consulted my father, the RSM and at the time QM* of the Gibraltar Regiment, about my intentions of joining the Regiment. I must have though, casually, as a matter of fact; after all he had been in the Army for more than 30 years.

When I say the Regiment is one big family, I mean it! Fathers, sons, brothers, cousins, and many women too. The influence of those who have served in the ranks of the Regiment is felt profoundly through Gibraltar; Chief Ministers, politicians, Lord Mayors, police, fire brigade, customs, and many other institutions and prominent individuals. Our Regiment unites and connects its members with the society we serve.

It was summer of 1983, I was 19 and I suppose that my number was up! Destiny, fate, or just a magnetic attraction to the service. I had lived through many military days, my mum would take us to every parade, fond memories of my father in brass buttoned ceremonial gear. The sound of the drum beating a military tattoo resounded in my bones, not something that can easily be escaped!

*Quartermaster.

In December 2014 I attended the 30th anniversary reunion of 10 Platoon, Salerno Company at the Royal Military Academy, Sandhurst. Seeing my old comrades reminded me how young and full of ideas we once were.

One of the fellows remains in the army, the others had new civy careers. Only one unemployed retired officer present, myself!

Day 74: Los Barrios to Campamento – 17 km

Morning. Matt accompanied me on a country track cutting across to la Estación de Los Barrios. Walked on alone over the little pseudo Roman bridge, past La Vega del Golf. This was all familiar territory. Crossed the motorway, a short walk on the Nacional and past the bar Rotunda. Back roads now, past Carteia, the ancient pre-Roman settlement, and past the monstrosity of la refinería, a sea side oil refinery. Many locals work there, the stench of fumes and chemicals make the whole area unbearable.

Got a call from Canal Sur Radio for a brief interview. They wanted to cover the walk on television and we arranged to meet later on. Over the bridge to Puente Mayorga, through Campamento, three cyclists passed and one shouted "Mark!" It was Ian House, a life-long friend, with Peter Ignacio and Derek Hernandez. They had recently been cycling the French Pyrenees in aid of charity.

Continued to the limits of La Línea de la Concepción where I met a film crew from Canal Sur TV. Walked a bit further, meeting my dad for the first time since I started. We had a couple of beers and later Mich picked me up, returned to Los Barrios. Phone rang – Gini from BFBS Radio Gibraltar calling for a brief interview which I gladly gave.

Day 75: Campamento to Gibraltar – 15 km

Could stretch out and touch the Rock. Cast my mind back to April, to the gun salute in Cardiff. Had I really been away that long – 75 Days? I would cross the frontier walk around, go home, and that's that. Unreal!

It had been an incredible journey through amazing places, meeting fascinating people. Wanted more, so much more! Should I turn around? A knot in the pit of my stomach, excited to be back home, but knew it was the end, the curtain call to my adventure.

Joined by Tammy and Francis Brancato, we started where I'd left off yesterday, at the edge of La Línea. At 0935 hrs crossed into Gibraltar. The final stamp for my credential from the immigration desk, bold black lettering declaring ARRIVED, FRONTIER. A GBC TV camera crew were filming and Customs, led by Tito Danino, another regimental officer, gave me a very warm welcome. Stepped out and was greeted by family and friends. James Gracia lay in ambush with a number of troops just out of sight.

Made our way round the east-side of the Rock. Must have been fifty of us. At Europa Point we stopped and took a group photograph. Proceeded through Rosia Bay and Jumpers, direction of Number 6 Convent Place – Chief Minister's Office.

Joined by the Military Historical Re-enactment Group, sporting Gibraltar Defence Force uniforms, looking very spiffy indeed!

Hugging my wife – back on British soil

Europa Point, Gibraltar

Met by our Chief Minister, Fabian Picardo, outside Number 6. Felt an immense sense of belonging and homecoming to my Regiment and to Gibraltar. Exchanged a few words and Fabian joined the march, carrying his eldest son. On my other side was Samantha Sacramento, who'd been in Cardiff for the gun salute. As we advanced down tourist packed Main Street the Pipes and Drums of the Lowland Band, together with our own band, formed up facing us. Drum Major stepped forward, saluted, welcomed me home.

I was pushing back the tears, felt perhaps for the very first time in the whole walk a real sense of achievement. We marched the length of Main Street behind the band and, at the Piazza Commander British Forces Gibraltar, the Commanding Officer, and members of the Regimental Council greeted the parade. Many stopped to shake my hand and say hello and well done!

My last few steps, the band came to a halt at Casemates. We stood nailed to the ground as the Drum Major about-turned, said a few words. and gave the order; "Scotland the Brave, for Colonel Randall!"

I was home.

Wished the pipes would never end.

With Chief Minister Fabian Picardo, his son Sebastian, and Drum Major Colour Sergeant D. Nelson

The Day After – Gibraltar

"C'mon, wake up." 0730 hrs. Tammy's blasted Latino alarm must have been reactivated, as she was dragging me out of bed at silly hour. "You've been round the Rock now we go up to the top, remember Ultreia! Forward and upwards!" What could I say? What could I do? Got up, got on my walking sandals, and got on with it.

At the top the levanter cloud raced over the edge and slammed against the rock face. Tammy said, "how does it feel?" I replied, "like I had never left!" She said, "well, vamos. A swim at Rosia y después to el supermarket, there is a 25% offer on all wines if you buy six bottles!"

Felt like singing, felt like dancing, felt like everything was right in the world and I could shout and yell and roar with joy. Instead, I went home to my family, cracked open a bottle of red, sat down on the couch, put Gladiator on, and got stinking drunk.

But don't tell anyone.

8

Epilogue

"Since the day of my birth, my death began its walk. It is
walking toward me, without hurrying."

~Jean Cocteau~

October 2009, Camino Francés. Tobias, the Austrian I met
in a bar a month earlier, had spoken about 'the obstacles we
find on the way'. I came to understand that the impediments
he faced were not material, but mountains of the soul,
barriers he had erected. He walked a path of inner anguish,
of deep seated insecurities. He had, as had I, built walls
around the heart.

I was brought up believing in original sin, Adam and Eve,
inheriting the sins of our fathers. This is at the core of a
Christian influenced upbringing, an unspoken nucleus of
western civilization and culture. We nurture this guilt, hide
our true sentiments from others, and ultimately from
ourselves. On my own for so long I confronted my demons,
with every step observed changes to the world around me
and to the world inside.

My mental meanderings were interrupted by the voice of
another pilgrim; "so what do you make of all this?" The older
man smiled, speaking in a sonorous French accent. I replied
"I don't know, I'm trying to let it sink in."

We continued on the path together, soon lost myself in
thought. Halting, looking around, realized I hadn't seen my
aged companion for over half an hour. Looked back down the
road, searched for some signs of life. Had he stopped? Given
up? I just waited for a sign.

He appeared! René, a 74 year old French pilgrim and retired postmaster, was suffering far more than I. Drenched in sweat, breath ragged, his face red and twisted into a frown. René smiled and collapsed as gracefully as as a proud man can.

He was exhausted, dehydration set his head spinning. Saw his desperation, frustration, his will to endure! Resting for a short while, René recuperated and we pushed on together for another 10 km.

That evening we sat by the front garden of a rustic albergue, a roaring fire fending off the evening chill. I told René what Tobias had said; "everything changes and stays the same, we have to learn how to overcome the obstacles we find on the way." I understood the changes and the obstacles, but was unsure of what he meant by things 'staying the same.'

René contemplated for a moment, responding cheerfully "ah, you see mon ami, in life all things are ever on the move! We are born, we work, we grow old! You will soon have a wrinkled up face, like me." René laughed and pinched his cheek.

"But, I am the same René that was squeezed from his mamas belly so many years ago, walking the same earth and swimming the same seas. Yes, yes, the world changes in a thousand small ways every day, but –"

René leaned back, his eyes meeting mine. "We're still using our tongues, our words! No matter how far you go, how long you travel, people have the same needs, live and breath and die in the same ways. Let me tell you this, a saying I have kept very close to my heart for many years, it goes; 'O God, give us the serenity to accept what cannot be changed, the courage to change what can be changed, and the wisdom to know the one from the other'. Beautiful, no?"

René stared into the embers of the dying fire. "The one thing Tobias wanted to change could never change. His family was dead and nothing would bring them back. His journey must be one of acceptance."

On the Camino we are all the same, have the same needs, the same focus unites us – getting to Santiago. The act of walking the same road day after day peels away layers of inhibition, of the masks we put on for others. You come to realise that happiness is not dependent on any one or anything else, being happy is a choice only you can make for yourself. If there is one lesson that I have taken from every Camino it is, very simply, be true to yourself.

I look back with fondness, deeply proud of my achievements. Every Camino is filled with rich memories, unique experiences. Cardiff to Gibraltar – Walk to the Rock, has had a profound effect on my life.

René told me of a French journalist who wrote about the world spinning due to the amount of pilgrims walking the Camino de Santiago, making it go round with their walking poles.

If that were only true!

The Real Story

As It Really Happened
Really!

9

A Café Somewhere in Gibraltar

Mark: "It's all a lie, you've got to believe me!"

Matt: "What is?"

Mark: "All of it, all, every last word. A lie. I couldn't, you see? I can't just tell the truth there," he brought the cup of coffee to his mouth slurping noisily. "You were there, and Tammy, and Francis, and James! Hell, everyone in Gibraltar was there!"

Matt: "I know. For the parade – we all walked up Main Street and the band played. It was nice."

Mark: "No, no, no – not for that! For the Battle! The Great Battle for Gibraltar!"

Matt: "We went to the reception after, right? You even gave a speech."

Mark: "Look, you're not listening to me. None of that matters – I'm trying to get at the truth here, listen," he leaned in lowering his voice. "That's just the surface stuff," he waved his hands, "the bits that we think we see with our eyes. I'm talking about the truth that we see with our hearts!" He finished with a flourish jabbing me viciously in my chest.

Matt: "You mean the stuff with the cows and the pigs – with the fighting and swimming through wine. That was real?"

Mark: "The truth! Reality as it is!"

Matt: "Nonsense."

Mark: "I swear – I was there! You've read it on Facebook, no?" He fixed me with a hard glare. "And if its on Facebook it must be true, right!"

Matt: "Well..."

Mark: "You've read it, right? I've been trying to get the truth out, disguised as a story – its important!"

Matt: "I've seen the titles. I've heard some rumours. You know, well, it seems a little strange."

Mark: "I know! I know – I can't help that. We need to get it out there – people need to know the truth! What Really Happened."

Matt: "You mean, apart from all the walking?"

Mark: "Well, and the frightful Friesians, the savage elite Pata Negra, the deadly Nazarenos, and –"

Matt: "And all the cheese and wine and more wine, right? Bloody rivers of wine – I think you could've swam your way down from Santiago."

Mark: "– the Ark, and of course, the most important thing! The Portrait of the Sandals-Grey!"

10

Mission The First

D-Day. Ok, not D-Day. Call it W-Day, for Walk Day, look, ok, just the day I started my walk then – right? Let me set the scene – Cardiff, grey skies, cannons to the left of me, cannons to my right. Before me the ancient stone walls of Cardiff Castle. The Royal Gibraltar Regiment, about ten of them, were stood to attention. This was the fabled gun salute from times of yore. I believe the very first gun salute ever was held right here by Julius Caesar himself, and later Wellington famously used a fifteen-hundred gun salute to drive Napoleon out of Europe.

This time it would only be a twenty-two gun salute, twenty-one of them in honour of Her Majesty, The Queen of England (God bless her soul) and a little gun – one, being fired south in my honour.

You wouldn't believe it but the Lord Mayor of the city of Cardiff emerged wearing a cunning disguise from behind a low hedge. "Psssst! Hey, pssssssst!" The Lord Mayor of the city of Cardiff called over to me. Yes, it was certainly the Lord Mayor. He wore a vermilion gown and had the golden keys to the gates of Cardiff hanging on a chain around his neck. What's vermilion? A type of ferret, google it. He, that being the Lord Mayor (lovely fellow once you get to know him), said unto me "Mark, pssst, hey Mark! A higher power has entrusted me to deliver to you this!" The Mayor parted his gown revealing a small wooden casket.

"What is it?" I asked, genuinely curious.

"This is the Ark of Cardiff!"

"Isn't it just a little wooden box?" I said.

The Lord Mayor tapped his nose, handing the box over. "Little do you know. You have been entrusted with the Ark, your sacred mission; to carry it, and the secret within, from here to Gibraltar. It holds your destiny, the entirety of your mission from hence forth shall be tied to the Ark!"

***

Matt: "Bollocks."

Mark: "Wait. I didn't say that,"

Matt: "No, I'm saying it. Me, Matt, the narrator. This is bollocks. None of it is real. I mean, I know you were in Cardiff but the rest of it? Meeting the Mayor, the whole bit about the gun salute. Wasn't it just the Queens Birthday thingy? And the Ark? C'mon. Its all bollocks."

Mark: "Don't interrupt, I've just got started." He snapped his fingers in the air summoning a waiter to our table. "Two carilladas, three montaditos, a bottle of your finest tinto, and una tapita of jamón serrano with cheese, por favor." He looked at me, "will you be wanting anything?"

***

~The Master Plan~

The Plan was simple – you know it? Been planning for months, researching, pouring over guidebooks and maps. Every inch of the way had been examined – the whole way, every kilometre from Cardiff down to Plymouth, across the Bay of Biscay, to Santander, on to Oviedo, to Santiago, and then! And then the length of the Iberian Peninsular to home

149

– home! All that way, all that planning – you know what I always say about the best laid plans of mice and men? That's right, there is always a bugger that throws a wrench into the works.

A thunderous roar of gunfire shook the earth and walls, the starters gun! I was off, like a hound after the tail of a fleeing hare – first Newport, then the M48 down the Severn Estuary. A fine start, brisk winds at my back up onto the Severn Bridge and across the fast flowing waters – all quite normal, right? Well, most of what I wrote for the diary holds true here, apart from a very significant incident with a Druid in Cheddar. Ahem. Well, walked through Bristol, walked sprawling business parks, busy roads, back alleys, and out into the countryside, advancing at a steady pace.

The Cheddar Gorge, a natural choke point. Risky business you might think, but then I didn't really consider myself at risk. Saw the bluffs, imagined a myriad of foes positioned on them, saw the dead ground and white stone boulders. Behind every bush could lurk a band of bandits! But there weren't. What's my point? Nothing, it was peaceful, that's my point – blueish skies, light winds, warm Cornish pasties, thick slices of cheese, and room temperature beer. Heaven on earth. That was, until I met The Druid.

~OOOooooOOOO its The Druid~

Mentioned him to you before, right? Only just now? Well, hells bells son, The Druid. Trust me son, it is a capital T in the for him. Bold as a full moon in the blackest night, I saw him first striding over hill and dale, vaulting a turnpike without breaking stride. He wore a fine grey beard almost down to the ground, a bird nest complete with speckled eggs in his hair, a long rough woven wicker robe that creaked tremendously as he moved, and thumped the earth at every stride with his thick oak staff (with a knob on the end).

The Druid approached, like a billowing storm and tsunami rolled into one. I stopped dead in my tracks watching him, he'd fixed me with an evil eye you see, held me in place with a mighty gaze. I'd nowhere to run! At the time I was deep in the folded lands of the Cheddar Gorge – beautiful place really, he'd come out of the wild, out of god knows where.

Following him must've been more than a hundred beady eyed sheep, whole squadrons appearing all of a sudden-like on the hills and ridges. He spoke, The Druid;

"Hello pilgrim. I've been expecting you." The Druid's voice was deep and sonorous. He spoke again – "here," towards me in his hands he held a plate with several slices of cheese. "The finest Cheddar, you must partake pilgrim."

"Thank you much-ly," I said. "Very nice indeed. Strong stuff. Any chance of a little wine to go with it?" The Druid shook his head, his wicker vest creaking. He looked me straight in the eyes – two black holes that bore right through me – he said again;

"Good stuff, eh?" Spoke The Druid.

"It is indeed." I replied, savouring the sweet and tangy taste of the well matured Cheddar.

"You'll find, pilgrim, that it is more than just good. In the days that come, through wind and rain, through every measure of hardship," The Druid pounded the earth with his staff, raising a hand into the air. "You'll find the taste that takes you from this world, that walks through shadow and grey skies." There was silence, an oppressive silence in which I could only hear and feel The Druid's deep voice sounding in my bones, raising every hair on my skin. "Keep true, keep honest, keep the Ark close to your heart – the true path shall reveal itself!"

Picture it, one moment it was clear. I stood before The Druid eating cheddar cheese in Cheddar Gorge surrounded by sheep, then the world flashed black and there I was, but he was gone. The Druid, gone! Vanished. Left the Cheddar Gorge, continued on my way, what else could I do?

The rest of my time in the UK passed pretty much like I've described in the diary – met up with Tammy, crossed the moors of Dartmoor, its in the name, no? And soon thereafter I got to Plymouth. With the passing of days I came to accept the apparition of The Druid as just that – an apparition. Perhaps a delusion brought on by a bad bit of cheese, maybe a mirage like those seen in the deserts – whatever, I was reluctant at the time to accept it as real.

~The Magnificent Golden Hind~

That is, the ferry from Plymouth to Santander – I boarded in the morning ready for a twenty-four hour journey across the Bay of Biscay. We left in a deep fog on calm seas – the fog persisted through the day and night. I spent some time in my cabin resting and up on the deck, watching the gulls circle overhead and Game of Thrones on my phone.

After walking for several days I felt warmed up, ready for the road ahead. At that time – I remember – it was twilight. Strange, it was twilight, but I can't remember quite if it was evening or morning... well, it was between day or night aboard the Golden Hind, in a thick soup of fog on a calm sea when.. when...

***

Matt: "When what?"

Mark: "I... I don't know." He took a deep gulp of his red
        wine. "I can't explain – when 'it' happened. You
        know in the X-Files when the aliens stop a plane in
        mid-flight and kidnap someone – well, it was some
        scary shit, something you'd expect out of the
        Bermuda Triangle."

Matt: "What happened? Where did the spooky aliens touch
        you?"

Mark: "Don't laugh. Please, I'm serious – listen, don't
        interrupt. I don't know what happened, but the
        world shifted. One moment I was here, well, there
        aboard the ferry crossing the Bay of Biscay, the next
        moment I was here. No, there. No, well, I moved –
        wait, no, the world moved around me. Ah hell!
        Waiter! Another bottle of tinto, por favor!"

11

Mission The Second

Dawn – grey skies on grey seas. The Golden Hind drew up to grey cliffs and the port city of Santander. I wore grey, at the far end of the gang-plank was a familiar face wearing a red jacket – the confirmatory visual sign of our alliance – matching our regimental colours.* Alighting from the ship I stumbled on the gang-plank and at that moment I recognised a friendly voice call out "Steady!"+ Clearly and firmly, delivered as an order; replied with "all's well!"± Francis, once my Commanding Officer and the CO of the Gibraltar Regiment, was waiting for me. I'd barely reached the shore when he lunged forward, grabbing my shoulders and pulled me into a back alley.

"Listen carefully," Francis said. "I will say this only once!"

"What is it Francis?" I replied.

"You are in trouble Mark, a deep ocean of trouble." Francis walked me to the other end of the alley.

"Trouble? What sort of trouble? Has something happened to my family?"

"No." He shook his head.

"You're pulling my leg. Is it the regiment? Has something happened to the lads?"

---

*Red and grey – scarlet for the infantry, grey for the limestone of the Rock.
+Countersign used by British troops during the Sortie from Gibraltar – 1781.
±Response by the Port Sergeant, custodian of the keys, when handing these back to the Governor. Full response is "Your Excellency, the fortress is secure and all's well."

"No, not that at all." Francis stopped before a large square door with big black brass knockers. "Inside, quick before we're seen!"

"Don't tell me, they've uncovered our copy of the real Treaty of Utrecht?" I gasped.

"Worse. Here, drink this." Francis ordered two bottles of wine, quickly downing a glass.

~The Trouble~

Francis spoke; "you have it, don't you? I know you do, as do they – the enemy!" He filled his glass from the bottle, glancing around at the other bar patrons and leaning in conspiratorially. "Malloy! Word has spread – everyone knows it! He knows!"

"Come on Francis, what the devil has got into you? Knows what? I haven't a clue what you're on about mate – are you sure you're up to walking with me?"

"Mark, for gods sake – listen! The Mayor of Cardiff – he gave you, ah er, it! Didn't he? It – you know, oh for christsakes – the Ark! The Ark of Cardiff!"

"Yeah, sure he did. Here, I've got it in my rucksack."

"No! Don't bring it out. Oh ye gods – Mark, do you not know what you've got there? The Ark! The whole of Iberia is your enemy! Thank the Saints that the CO sent out a press release claiming you'd be alighting at Calais, else you'd have been met by the Guardia Serrano* at the docks!"

"Sorry, what? Iberia? Guardia Serrano?" I looked at my half imbibed glass of red wine, lifting it to my nose and giving it a

*Iberia's half human, half porcine police force, as I was later to discover.

good sniff – nothing seemed out of order. "Francis, slow down – I've no idea what you are talking about."

"Some things never change." Francis said.

"Sorry, what?"

"We have to move quickly! Quick! Only time for one more bottle and a couple of tapitas, have to be on the road before they realize we're here!" Francis jumped to his feet. "But first! Where's the pisser?"

~Close Encounters of a Spooky Sort~

On my own again, sipping a glass of red and mulling over my old friends words – strange, so very strange. Like that episode of the X-Files where Mulder lures Scully onto his water-bed – something was askew.

The barman was polishing a glass held firmly between two trotters. I looked around – down the bar was an old tusked boar sipping a decaf, very strange, why decaf? The doors to the ladies swung open – a cow on its hind legs strolled out, wearing a blue set of overalls.

"!" I thought. And "!!" again. Animals! Beasts wearing clothes! You must know, my first reaction was to look to my cup of wine – had I been drugged? Had some passing hippy/CIA agent slipped nefarious hallucinogens into my drink?

A small bristle backed porcine wearing a blue summer dress was led by the hand by her mother, a bulbous swine in a straw hat. She saw me staring at them, slack jawed and glassy eyed, turned up her snout at me and snorted! Can you believe it? Snorted at by a swine in a straw hat!

I thought I was going quite mad, you know, entirely bonkers – but... but well, maybe I did go a little mad for a time, just a little bit. You cannot imagine the relief I felt when the bathroom door swung open and Francis emerged – fully human, wiping his hands on his shirt. The sheer relief I tell you, palpable!

We set off – down the Camino del Norte, two undercover retired military officers. Using our full expert knowledge, honed by years of experience, to sniff out, uproot, to fully discover every bar, taberna, and cafetería that lay hidden on the Camino. We were to pretend to be purveyors of fine wines and sidra, moving stealthily from bodega to sidreria along the Cantabrian and Asturian coast. We fully imbibed in the atmosphere. Fully.

I'd continued to see these animals all around – normal creatures walking and talking and doing all the things that people do – could the crafty Cantabrian canteen owners be spiking our drinks? Was Francis seeing the same things as I?

***

Matt: "Hold it, hold it right there. Animals wearing clothes? Walking upright? This sounds very.. very Animal Farm to me."

Mark: "No, no, no – why of course not! Nothing like that at all!"

Matt: "Really?"

Mark: "Truly – there is no deeper significance behind these animalistic appearances at all, none!"

Matt: "Hmm. Alright, if its you saying it its kinda believable."

Mark: "Regardless – this is the truth! Animals and all, reality!"

***

~The Nostro-Hammond Experience~

After several pleasant nights and days of walking and talking, Francis said something that I found to be a little odd – a little jarring. We were talking about the hardships of walking day in day out and he said; "yes, I agree Mark. It is just like Nostro-Hammond predicted."

"Nostro-Hammond?" I replied. Who do you mean? You mean Hammond the singer-songwriter?"

"Of course!" Francis said, continuing "Our Seer of Gibraltar, Nostro-Hammond. He said unto me that I would be a part of a trial, that it would be a hardship I must endure – that we must endure together. It is all pre ordained Mark, it is written. In the stars, you know?" He pointed up at the sky.

"Its day time." I said.

"The stars are still out at day, just you cannot see them. Anyway, the sun is a star too."

"I don't see anything written in the sun."

"You're not a seer Mark, you have to have special seer eyes to see that kind of thing." said Francis.

We reminisced on our training days, remembering the words of the four wise men from Merseyside. They'd warned of 'the long and winding road that leads to your door'. They'd not said how long it would be, or how much we would drink!

Following the signs; little arrows painted in yellow (just like Nostro-Hammond predicted!) we walked some 40 kilometres. I detail the mundane stuff in my diary, you've read that right? Right, good – well, most things seemed somewhat normal. I was walking in a dream through familiar roads, like the world had suddenly shifted several inches to the left and everything was the same but different. The things that should be the same were – I mean, cars and planes and roads, churches and towns – indistinguishable!

But, every now and again Francis would grip my arm and pull me aside as a patrol of Guardia Serrano marched by, the patrols were getting more and more frequent – looking for me!

In the watering holes of the northern Spanish coast we drank oblivious to the dangers of alcohol poisoning. Following the signs and well trod paths we made good progress.

One fine Cantabrian day we came across a pilgrim of Germanic stock sprawled out across a bridge. It was a simple matter, with our military recognitions skills, to distinguish his nationality at a glance; long white tube socks, alpine boots, and lederhosen somewhat gave the game away.

"Agua, agua por favor." He was of advanced age and in luck. Our copious consumption of local beverages meant that we'd plenty of water to share. His words were incoherent, saying "achtung! Es ist eine bombe auf der brücke!"* Laughing, he exclaimed "das machinen icht kaputten!"+

After almost five years in Germany all I could manage was "ein bier bitte." He reacted, getting up and struggling along with us. It seemed that the Iberians had been spiking his drink; we uncovered a treacherous plot! He had been tricked into believing that Francis and I were fleeing chorizo thieves and was left behind by his compatriots to slow our advance. His reserve demolition plans had been foiled – the device a string of morcilla tied together with copper wire!

*Attention! There is a bomb on the bridge!
+The machine is kapputten!

159

I had in my heart a cunning plan. They'd expect me to take the most direct route from Oviedo to Leon, but I was no fool! Aha! Too easy, no? It was the masterful 'Stifling Plan'? Inspired by the 'Schlieffen Plan', similar to how the Wehrmacht swung right through Belgium to avoid the Maginot Line, I would right-flank the mountains of Asturias and avoid the main resistance in León, base of the X Legion.

To do so I would head inland, cross the mountains through to Oviedo along the Asturian highlands – that brought its own set of dangers, but I would be less likely to be discovered if I kept to these solitary paths.

At this time I still walked in a half dream state, perhaps not taking all that was occurring as seriously as I should have. I'd seen many creatures since meeting Francis, every morning I awoke expecting, well, normality I suppose. Did I mention Tineo in the diary? No? Only in passing?

It was on the third day after parting with Francis that I came to a mist filled valley. Blue skies above, I descended from the high ridge into a swirling twilight world that ended at the edge of the path.

In this small sightless world I walked – forward, following the stony path down by a quick flowing stream that slow became a river, black water over smooth stones. The dirt paths changed to cobblestone and ahead I heard the sounds of a town.

12

Mission The Third

A year ago I had traversed the route known colloquially as the Camino San Salvador, a short cut through the high mountain passes separating Asturias from Castilla y León. My morale high; they'd expect me this way again to crash and burn at their solidly constructed line of defence – Ha! The French made the same mistake with the Magi-not Line! My 'Stifling Plan' in motion, I blitzed through the familiar terrain for a few days. Revelling in my superior cunning, how I had once again supremely outwitted the foe.

~Night of the Fat Udders~

The fiendish X Legion lay in ambush in the high mountain passes between Oviedo and Lugo, at Tineo they struck! Hiding in the shadows and alleyways, as I walked past a toyshop they pounced! A rampage of hooves and hob nailed boots screeching on cobblestone. By a thousand furious black-horned beasties I was surrounded, ensnared, entrapped, en, uh, great danger. I had been outwitted by a herd of crazy cows! Alas, no plan survives initial contact with the enemy.

They dragged me to the lobby of a hotel called Calvario. There I met my nemesis. Ambushed, bound, gagged, and tied to bed of springs. A huge hooded figure in a menacing black leather garb connected two wires to the bed springs – it was just like in Rambo 3! I could only writhe in agony as the thousands of volts shot through, charring my flesh like a forgotten sausage in the corner of a grill.

Outside the herd assembled for the kill, low braying at first, the moo-ing commenced; some applauded, others shouted olé! They ransacked my rucksack, spilling my maps and emergency golf balls onto the road. Then, then! They held my mouth open as the ugliest of them, with the biggest udders I'd ever seen, forced her teats between my clenched teeth and squirted creamy, fresh milk down my throat.

Amongst them one heifer stood out, head and shoulders above the rest. She had even larger milk laden udders, wielded a pointed broadsword, and wore upon her speckled brow an iron wrought helmet with fancy feathered wings. The cattle gathered round her calling out "Freda! Freda!"

Freda wore a hefty gold chain bearing the symbol of the Chieftain of the Friesian tribe – two snakes coming together over a milk churn. She walked to the forefront, sword in hoof entering into the Calvario. Was this the end, was I to be skewered and left to rot?

~Rambo: First Milk~

Freda upended my rucksack, the Ark fell out. She clutched the box in her trotters holding it aloft. "I have the Holy of Holies!" Freda yelled. The herd wild and snorting stampeded through the town streets in a triumphant trot. "And now!" Freda raised the casket above her. "We shall reveal the secret of the Ark! La leche de Asturias will be the only milk! We shall expand to all markets and force our leche merengada and arroz con leche* to be the staple food for all! Hail Friesia! The Leche-Reich will last ten thousand years!"

"Hold on!" From the other side of the square a voice called out – "don't do it Freda! Malloy wants the Ark delivered intact!"

*Milk based desserts.

"Malloy? Pah," Freda squirted a half cup of milk out on the ground in disgust. "Dass alte morsche wurst?* The Ark shall not be wasted on a schweinehund like Malloy – It belongs to the Friesians!" A triumphant roar erupted from the assembled Legion X.

Strapped to the metal bed and feeling more than a little soiled, bloated, and defeated, I sincerely thought that my mission was at its end.

A silence fell upon the assemblage as Freda cracked open the Ark. A warm wind rose and flowed towards the open box, the air grew thick with a purple fog. Like thunder, a bright blinding flash exploded out from where Freda stood. I heard the brass clank of cow bells, the clattering of hoofs and a hellish agonizing moo.

Silence.

The tantalizing scent of roast beef!

My shackles snapped open, falling to the ground. The streets lay littered with charcoaled charcuterie of dozens of the horned black and white marked fiends, enough to fill a butcher's window several times over! From the burnt black hooves of the very barbecued heifer, Freda, as dead as a well cooked beef sirloin, I retrieved the Ark of Cardiff and secreted it once more in my rucksack.

Snatching up a rack of barbecued ribs I fled town, following the yellow arrows south-west. The foe was now well aware of my current position, and of the extraordinary artefact I had been entrusted. This was a close call, too close for comfort. Another plan would be needed.

*That old rotten sausage?

163

~That Tall Nordic Look~

I would have to disguise myself as a Nordic pilgrim. Wearing Nordic wooden high-heeled sandals I would appear taller. I could speak Scandinavian, or at least pretend to. With a few remembered words, a simple greeting and goodbye – hallå and adjö, and a friendly reassurance in times of trouble – jag är inte en nazi spion.* And most of all I would have to change my name, em, eh, I would call myself Lladnar Kram. This could work, yes Lladnar Kram!

On the road again I met and greeted fellow pilgrims with a knowing "jag har en härlig par kokosnötter"+ Most greeted me with perplexed smiles, but their lack of response confirmed my disguise was working. It was to be several hard days of marching in wood clogs before I would see the grand citadel of Santiago de Compostela.

I took off my high-heeled sandals and put my worn and blistered feet in the cool waters of a nearby fountain, my thoughts turning to the journey ahead. A passer-by chucked some coins at me. At least I had some beer money.

*I am not a Nazi spy.
+I have a lovely pair of coconuts.

13
Mission The Fourth

~The Good, the Bad, and the Bufand~

I felt alone, abandoned on the road – more than a feeling. The cathedral bells chimed six times as I walked from the Praza do Obradoiro out of the saint's stronghold. I had already entered into the crypt below the main alter bearing witness to the dust and bones of Saint James Matamoros. Hundreds of thousands came every year to walk that narrow labyrinth and pay homage to the 'Slayer of Moors'.

My name became known – 'El Gran, the Great, Terminator of the Friesian clan'. Everywhere along the Camino were posters and newsletters with the crude portrait of a bearded freak. They must have used a picture of a discarded character from the Muppet Show, for it bore no resemblance whatsoever to my face. The only way that I knew they were after me and not some escaped freak of nature were by the words beneath:

Wanted

– Mark "Bufandboy"* Randall –

For Crimes Against the State

Signed: Cyriano Malloy

The Friesian clan had been almost entirely consumed by the Holy Fire. A few lucky survivors were under the watchful eyes of Galician overlords and as I traversed the fields of Arzúa I saw them put to hard labour in the production of

*Scarf-boy.

cheese. Feeling the stare of a thousand blood-thirsty eyes on me I hurried my pace.

The word had spread; the Camino was safe. Even with my crude depiction adorning a thousand albergues, I abandoned my disguise, mixing freely with my fellow pilgrims. My feet healed somewhat after shedding the wooden clogs.

On the road my eyes met with a number of pilgrims coming in the opposite direction, towards their final destination of Santiago de Compostela. There were several creatures amongst them, those upright half human inhabitants of this dream world – you've seen the film Kung Fu Panda? Bloody good flick, well – it was kind of like that, with them walking and talking and not being a shade short of human, except for the snouts and trotters and udders and well, all that.

I felt as if I'd fallen into a parallel world, I mean, I was the same, I am the same now! But everything is different, changed, become bizarre-o land. Have you seen Back to the Future 2? Well, it was just like that! Everything the same but different in strange and significant ways.

My foundation was slipping, I was slipping! I injured my foot, catching it on a pilgrim who'd fallen asleep in the middle of the road. He revealed his name to be Siothrún Akhenaten, an Irish- Egyptian pilgrim on his way to Santiago for a penance. In conversation over a couple of bottles of tinto he revealed to me that he was a Highlander, one of the Immortals from ancient times who had been given a mission by God to put together a sacred band and...

***

Matt: "Hold on. Hold it right there. Stop."

Mark: "What? What now?"

Matt: "This is too much – Rambo? Fine, I can accept that. But now you've just brought up four films in one go? Come on, you're just giving me the plot of Highlander mixed up with Blues Brothers." I found it hard, even as the narrator to credit what I'd just heard.

Mark: "No, not at all. This really happened. Would I lie to you?" He toyed with a chorizo on the end of his fork. It was getting to be late afternoon in the café.

Matt: "Well."

Mark: "Would I?"

Matt: "Yes, you would." And yes, he would too.

Mark: "Nonsense. I would never lie. Look, shut it. Stop interrupting. Who's paying the bill for this?"

Matt: "You are."

Mark: "Right. And you're listening to my story, so let me tell it, damn your eyes." He slammed his hand onto the table disturbing a plate of olives.

***

~The Portrait of Sandals-Grey~

Where was I? Oh right – on the road to Astorga. Right, right. I soon arrived at the ancient city of Astorga where the trade of silver baubles and el cocido mara-gato* dominate the populaces daily routine. There were a multitude of pilgrims bartering and procuring goods. Close by an artillery regiment was running drills and shooting at distant targets with indirect gunfire. Watched them for a time, but had to move on before it got too late.

*Traditional stew in Astorga, typically made with cats.

From a narrow alleyway a croaky voice called out; "Friend, have you any silver, shiny silver pieces to trade?" I turned, stepping on a cat. It shrieked attracting a Castilian cat-knapper who readily snapped it up, one for the cocido mara-gato!

The throaty voice appeared to belong to a crooked pilgrim haunched over on an equally crooked stave. She smiled a crooked smile and spoke with a warble. "Give me twelve pieces of silver and take this, a gift! Let no eyes other than your own fall upon it."

"If I need to pay, it isn't a gift." I said.

"Do not judge the value of this gift by the silver I ask amigo, the money is just for my bus fare!"

I took the gift of parchment from her hands, thinking it was a map or menu for a nearby restaurant, gave her the silver and moved on. Later sat in the vestibules of a coffee shop I unfurled the parchment. It read –

Herewith, a portrait of your sandalled feet.

Whilst the portrait survives your feet will never tire!

Let each step lead you on your way.

The artist was no ordinary scribbler – I instantly recognized the masterful strokes, delicate lines between the toes and dirt. A renown master! Renown amongst all who count the whole world over, delightfully giving life to any portrait and imbuing them with an indelible essence of vitality. His professional mark, the symbol of the early Christian - a fish, with a hook!

This parchment contained something phenomenal, a depiction of my sandalled feet, drawn with such force and potency that I feared they might march off the paper and down the street!

An incredible asset; a force multiplier which would grant an edge over any and all potential foes. I could walk non-stop for days, uphill, on the hardest tarmac, through forests, cross rivers, cross gorges, downhill, up mountains. Just by holding it near me my feet would never age; the art would absorb all my ills. Precisely what an infantry soldier needs.

The Ark with the message for Gibraltar was still in my custody. Was this portrait a gift from the heavens, or had I sold the souls of my soles to the horned beast in disguise? Was this a chorizo ploy to discredit me? Could unseen dangers lurk between the lines of the Portrait? Doubt filled my mind, gripped my heart. My feet were itching to move. No more blisters, no more pain. I would eat up the kilometres, either way – what a fantastic gift!

14

Mission The Fifth

~Pork's Drift~

A thin beam of light pierced through the dark. Behind I could hear the sound of running water. The days had been hard on my feet and on my spirit. Had to dodge enemy patrols, avoid inebriated poachers, and worst of all – survive on only one bottle of red a day! But! There was a ray of sunshine in my ordeal, you see, for I no longer walked alone!

Tammy had flown in from her training with Exeter University Officer Training Corps. Before, some twenty-four hours previously, we'd conspired together to cross, and if necessary destroy the bridge on the River Caray. It was a desperate measure, a last ditch effort you might say.

My circumstances had become a little, shall we say, complex? Yes, complex. That's a good word – right. Leaving the ancient city of Astorga I spied several porcine Guardia Serrano at a checkpoint. Too late to turn back or seek another route. In a gruff voice they demanded "papers, por favor!" And I complied, handing over my passport. What a fool! I should have run! I should have done a thousand things different that I did not do!

In a thrice they had me surrounded – I held up my walking sticks, they knocked them aside with a single swipe of their trotters. I struggled – mightily! They had me by the rucksack, with greasy morcilla truncheons they savagely clobbered me. Look, you can see the bruising even now here on my head. Trussed up, thrown into the back of a black windowed van – I was done for! How careless had I been!

But!

An explosion! Boom! An eruption of earth and tarmac! The whole world shuddered for a moment and was still. Outside I heard a motorcade, the sound of drums and music. Approaching was a military artillery convoy performing training exercises near Astorga. They had spied my predicament from afar and hastened to my aid.

I saluted – astounded – were the military at my side? The answer was rather obvious, as soon as the lead vehicle approached I saw Tammy, and the Exeter Officer Training Corps with her, on a special undercover mission! Incredible, I know, right? Yeah, completely unbelievable, I wouldn't credit it either – unless you had lived it.

~The Bridge Over the River Caray~

Checkpoints had been set up the length and longth of la Vía de la Plata. Tammy informed me that Malloy and his nefarious sidekick, the Seacock, were acting openly against us. There were rumours of an embargo on the Rock, and worse! Whispered in the secret bodegas throughout Iberia was a single word – "asedio."*

I was not to know this at the time, of course. With Tammy at my side progress was faster than ever. We played on each others strengths and covered for our weaknesses – but, there was a place, a stretch of the road that could not easily be traversed. A place that our foes knew we must cross – and cross we must! That is, the bridge over the River Caray.

We lay up in the pre-dawn dark waiting for the right moment. Tammy had specially formulated a communications plan – she'd been trained to build a

*Siege.

sophisticated walkie-talkie. I was unaware of the technical specifications of the contraption, but saw it involved two empty tins of evaporated milk, opened at one side, tied together by a long piece of string – the latest in British military technology!

"Dad, top men have been working on this for years", she enthused. "You affix one can over your ear and talk. Then we reverse the process when you talk. Incredible, no?"

I shook my head and sighed. "We really are living in the future." Certain of the devices reliability, I firmly attached one of the cans to the side of my head.

"Hallo Mike Romeo, this is Tango Romeo, over." I heard the crackle of the signal passing through the string as if from a great distance.

"Tango Romeo," I replied, "this is Mike Romeo. Please confirm your location, over."

"Mike Romeo, you are five feet from me, over."

"Roger Tango Romeo, I can hear you loud and clear, out." We had only managed to procure a short length of string.

"Is that you dad? I can hear a rasping noise." Tammy looked around. I was scratching like a dirty dog on a lazy day. "Stop scratching, it's interfering with communications."

A few days earlier in an albergue I had chanced upon a troupe of Romany circus fleas. The entire performing cast snuck aboard whilst I slept and hitched a free ride to the south on my lower legs.

To our front lay the bridge on the River Caray. In a corner of a fenced field huddled together in a circle, were the squad of Benavente, waiting in silence and determined to impede our progress. We'd not been seen – working as a pair, we'd have to cross the field silently, undetected. I instructed Tango

Romeo to extend her walking poles and unsheathe the sharp metal tips.

This was serious opposition. All had previous experience from past fiestas, sharp horns, and were black as coal; the fearsome 'All Blacks'. From the Astorga based artillery we received word of operational support. A FOO,[*] codename "Rocky-Five" was prepared to call gunfire on the enemy positions on our behalf.

I held the communications can to my mouth, cast a stern glance at Tammy, took a deep breath and delivered the traditional Royal Gibraltar Regiment pre-battle speech.

"Three weeks from now I will be at the Piazza drinking coffee. Imagine where you will be, and it will be so – Hold The Line! Stay With Me! If you find yourself alone lying on a rocky cove, with the sun on your face, do not be troubled. For you are in El-Kwari[+] fighting for a table and you're already dead – At my signal unleash hell."

Tammy closed in and whispered, "Dad, dad, the string snagged, what were you saying?"

I gave the signal to advance in a line, the two of us abreast. Scratched again, a thin red line run down the sides of my legs. The All Blacks had seen us almost immediately – our approach had been spied by a solitary scout and with a low warning bray our position betrayed.

Too late to leg it. We were surrounded, a tight wedge formation from the flank, three skirmishers appearing from dead ground. We feinted west, rapidly turning and dodging through a thicket, over a turnpike and south towards the bridge.

---

*Forward Observation Officer.
+Sea side bear pit where the elderly fight over tables and umbrella space.

Over the Bridge! The other side of the River Caray, that was the answer! That was where safety lay! Tammy stumbled, I caught her but failed to maintain balance – we both went over, falling to the dirt and long grass. A roar – a menacing long mooooo shook my heart. We were done for!

I opened my rucksack and unfurled the parchment holding it aloft. We were surrounded, there was little hope left – I could only pray for a miracle! Just as had happened many years before, when the banner of St James stained with blood had been flown leading Sharpe to defeat the French. I could only wave the Portrait of Sandals-Grey and pray!

"Dad! Quick, take this and give the order!" Tammy flung the communications device into my arms. Hesitating no longer I called the FOO, "final protective fire requested at my position!" It would be a risky gamble, like playing Russian roulette with a semi automatic – but it had to be done.

"Roger wilco, sending through the 'Matador' special munitions". Crackling through the battered tin came the reply.

I scrambled to my feet, Tammy had been injured – limping ahead like a wounded donkey. We dashed down the path, down the narrow slope and onto tarmac, stumbling together onto the bridge. All around were shapes – shadows, stamping hooves in half light getting closer. Tammy leaned on my shoulder, we backed up the road not daring to turn our backs on the beasts.

From the fields they came – a hundred or more toros bravos,* la crème de la crème. Each six foot tall with black glazed horns, waxed moustaches and golden rings on their noses. They formed a single column, Napoleon's Hammer! A

*Special breed of fighting bulls.

thumping of hooves, a ra-ta-ta-tat and with a thousand snorts enough to shake the very heavens.

We'd no hope. They had our number, had punched our ticket, our journey was surely at its end...

~Das Bomb~

There was a noise, a distant whistle and whirr of metal streaking through the skies. We looked up – there! The shell burst high in the sky, piercing through the low clouds and shrieking madly to the earth.

The All Blacks were caught out in the open in tight formation as destruction rained down on them. What a spectacle of colour and light. Inflatable matadors, in traje de luces,[*] sword in hand, floating down on their red capes.

The bulls were confused as the look-alike matadors struck. Some found their target immediately bringing them down in a stroke. Others begun showing off with their capes and then struck home. These were truly smart munitions! Over half the All Blacks had been decimated by artillery fire, their ears taken as trophies. Most withdrew, bloodied from the aerial corrida.[+]

We continued to advance. Tammy carried the Ark, I wore sandals-grey. A solitary toro bravo emerged from a side road, stamping its hooves and pointing its horns at me! Thought that with my sandals I would outrun it. Alas, cutting my hair on Tammy's advice had weakened me.

Kneeling, I dug the handle of my walking stick into the ground, offering the glittering point of my pole at the charging bull. Could feel it's warm breath on my face, when,

*Tight fitting attire worn by bullfighters.
+Bull fight.

most unexpectedly it collapsed to my front! Lying on its back, rolling around in the dirt, agonising. I saw that my troupe of circus fleas had taken up a new host and were already performing on him.

It was over, the All Blacks lay decimated on the field of battle.

What a victory.

We crossed the River Caray and headed south. Tammy and I parted ways where the road split to Salamanca. The path now lay open, flat fields and fat clouds floating in clear skies; I couldn't help but sing every hippie tune I knew – "If you're going to Sa-la-manca, be sure to wear a montera* on your head, la la la."

It would be another 800 kilometres to home, the equivalent of the entire Camino Francés from St Jean Pied de Port to Santiago. I had a hell of a long way to go, and only so many songs on my playlist left to do it in.

*Funny hat that bullfighters wear.

15
Mission The Sixth

The fog descended over Salamanca. Only the church spires and collegiate towers could be seen rising above the thick misty soup. I crossed the ancient Roman bridge, a pale silhouette clad in black robes and drawn hood some fifty paces behind. I knew I was being followed, knew that I had a stalker on my heels. There was nothing I could do, so I pressed on.

With the new sun the soup of fog cleared, like a thick gazpacho turning into a crystal clear consumé. At the day's end I took refuge at a road inn, quenching my thirst with chilled red wine. In the corner of the taberna I observed the self-same cloaked figure. His eyes met mine, baleful and filled with undisguised scorn. I motioned with a tilt of my head and he crossed to join me at my table.

"State your business," I growled in my best Russell Crowe impression. "Be brief. Speak quick, or I shall imprint the sole of my sandals on your backside!"

The man spoke and by the time he'd finished with his tale I was wiping away tears, not from anything he'd said mind, but from two jugs of red and the spicy chorizo. He didn't really talk all that long – I drink and eat fast!

~Tales of the Unrepentant~

Hans Cerezo del Valle del Jerte de Pizarro was the direct descendent of German pilgrims who had roamed the plains of Castilla y León in search of religious relics. Captured and enslaved by conquistadores of Extremadura during the time of Don Quixote, they now served their Iberian masters in every evil trade. They remained, wandering the vast mesetas without a fixed abode – these were the lost pilgrims.

In his eyes I saw a hope, an almost forlorn desire. Hans was one of the few who was forced to tend to herds of swine whilst the señores Extremeños went gallivanting to the Americas in search of silver and gold. He had formed an alliance of old families, los Defensores del Camino[*] – a society imbued with the values of a chivalric order. They caught wind of my undertaking – the struggle of good and evil in which I'd become embroiled. That is, the Ark of course – of my mission to bring the Holy Ark from Cardiff to its new resting place in Gibraltar. Hans leaned in and asked; "Is it true Mark? What they say about the Portrait of Sandals-Grey?"

He had a gleam in his eyes, hope, a desperate glint. I said "Yes Hans, it is true. It is a lovely painting."

Hans spoke; "I know I can trust in you, another chorizo? The key to our freedom Mark, is in the fortress city of Cáceres. There is a golden medallion that usually hangs on the neck of the Jefe de los Nazarenos, the foremost authority in penitente circles. I do not say these words lightly, but as a fellow walker on the path I must ask this of you! Please, you must go and steal the medallion from las hermandades de Nazarenos and Capirotes[+]. You who wield the Ark and the Portrait, who has defeated the X-Legion and triumphed over Malloy's All Blacks! Please Mark, you are our only hope!" Hans lifted a silver cross to his lips and kissed it. "For all that is holy, we are in desperate need!"

*Señores Extremeños – lords of Extremadura, Defensores del Camino – Defenders of the Way.
+Jefe de los Nazarenos – Chief of the Nazarenes, las hermandades de Nazarenos and Capirotes – brotherhood of the Nazaranes and pointy hoods.

I met his eyes, firm and unyielding and said "keep talking".

Hans bowed his head saying "thank you! Thank you!"

"I have decided nothing yet Hans," I said, though my heart was already steeled to go to Cácares.

Hans nodded, continuing; "they wear penitential robes and hoods with conical tips to conceal their identity. They are descended from the conquistadores and seek forgiveness for the horrors their ancestors inflicted on the indigenous people of las Américas. But these fools squandered their ability to produce jamón de bellota* and chorizo. They follow the symbol of our old family, that of the medallion. By recovering it I hope to reunite our tribes, to bring the pilgrims back on to the true path!"

I refilled his glass of wine, Hans said; "please be careful, take the medallion from their headquarters in Cáceres and my people will be freed."

He finished his drink, threw down a gold coin and left the tavern.

Hans had given me a mission I could not undertake on my own. Using the extensive communications knowledge Tammy had passed on, I hooked up a can to a telegraph pole and called the Commanding Officer of the Royal Gibraltar Regiment.

~Risqué Reinforcements~

"I have the perfect man for the job," the CO said confidently. "Sniper trained, climber, master of disguise, and hasn't stopped talking about budgets and health and safety since he took over as my 2IC."

*Ham from acorn fed pigs.

"Very good" I said.

The CO replied "James will meet with you in Cáceres a week and a day from now".

"How are things back home?" I asked. Knowing the line was not secure I dared not mention anything about the Ark of Cardiff.

There was silence on the line. I strained to listen but there were only cracking noises and a distant beep. "Things are fine Mark," came the belayed response from the CO. "Everything is good. Just fine. Get here safely. Good luck."

For a week I marched, covering extra long distances and surviving off a Spartan diet of jamón serrano, queso manchego, and vino tinto in order to make good my rendezvous in Cáceres.

In the interim I'd received a research package from Tammy on my new foes – the Nazarenos. They carry processional candles and rough-hewn wooden crosses, walk the city streets barefoot with shackles and chains on their feet as a penance. Every brotherhood distinguishes themselves by hauling magnificent pasos – floats adorned with sculptures depicting scenes from the ancient holy histories.

During this time I discovered something remarkable – I had spilled a drop of red wine onto the Portrait of Sandals-Grey and it flashed in a rainbow of colours. I spilled another drop, intentionally, and another – each time the parchment would flash and absorb the liquid. Holding it in my hands I felt an incredible energy pour through my fingers and up, into my head and the whole of my body – a vital force, filled with warmth and a gentle spirit – I felt I could walk forever!

Immediately ordered a dozen bottles of red, pouring a full bottle into the painting. Powered in this fashion the distances of the road held no meaning for me – I could walk 40, 50, even 60 kilometres in a single day!

~Where Seagulls Dare~

Whilst watering at a local dive in the Plaza Mayor I happened upon señor Celestino, a Centurión de la Guardia de Cristo y Nazareno de la Primera Orden.* He was one of them! I instantly hatched a cunning plan and begun plying him with the juice of the fruit of the vine. We became fast friends and he promised to take me to their HQ. Together we sang through the streets of Cáceres to an ancient stone arched building, where he helped me dress like a Nazareno. Pointy hat and rope belt and all, full of spirits we went through the paces. I was more than accustomed to a multitude of drills and marching under the influence whilst serving in the Regiment.

I secretly snapped several pictures of their deployment for the Semana Santa.+ The Nazareno High Command walked in, all cloaked and covered up. The Chief Nazareno wore the medallion! It glittered like a golden chorizo bathed in salsa picante. Around him stood several seven foot giants in sharp pointed hoods, their monstrous muscles formed from a lifetime of carrying the pasos. Could not risk this on my own, no way josé! Where was James when I needed him?

Gritting my teeth I crossed the plaza, getting as close to the group as I dared. I froze. A shiver run up, then down, and again up my whole spine. Felt something pressing into my lower back. There I stood for a whole minute. Slowly, not daring to make a single sudden movement, I turned

*Centurion Guard of Christ and Nazarene of the First Order.
+Holy week.

Behind me was a Nazareno, all in black. His eyes just visible through slits in the cloth. He winked once, then twice – Morse Code! It was James, truly a master of disguise. A sniper through and through, the elite of the elite, trained to conceal themselves, blend with their surroundings. James had done just that – he'd submerged himself, become one of them. How the devil did he get here before me?

Our eyes furiously blinked out a pattern in Morse Code.

Mission – take the medallion. James responded – scouted terrain – Cáceres narrow streets.

Situation – surrounded by Nazarenos. My eyelids felt heavy, but I persevered!

Execution – I would create a diversion – James to snatch medallion.

Coordinating Instructions – immediate action – imminent!

Blinked three more times and the plan was a-go!

~Dances with Wine~

With a fast cha-cha-cha I enacted stage one of our plan – the distraction. Out through the black door into the dressing rooms once more – oh, how they must have cursed me for an eternity up and down Iberia as I danced the infamous lambada. Jaws agape, screaming "Afuera pervertido, echarlo, quitarle los vestimientos!"*

James was as quick as a dik-dik that had seen a cheetah. The focus of the entire congregation was on my thrusting hip and scintillating hand movement. Did a quick half turn, stamped my foot like Fred Astaire and went on to la Macarena. They were more than impressed, I could tell by the way they

*Scram pervert, toss him out, remove his vestments!

gathered around and waved clubs in the air. One overly eager fan took a hold of me, thought him a dance partner and sang a few refrains of Boogie Nights. Another set of hands fell upon my hood, and another, and in no short order I was violently expelled from the building. The Nazarenos shouting "marchate desgraciado, eres un sinvergüenza!"*

James was nowhere to be seen.

Shed my disguise, hoofing it post-haste through the narrow alleys of the old Cácares. If James had succeeded in his part I knew that it wouldn't take too long for the Nazarenos to realize that the thieves would still likely be on the streets. The chase was on. Muffled clangs and clomping clogs echoed off the stone walls, the rattling of chains and drums beating in a frenzy was getting louder, closer. Was this a normal procession, or a hunt? The Nazarenos would flay me alive, burn me at the stake. Feet adorned with Sandals-Grey flopped fleetly on cobbled streets, fleeing desperate. The sound of drums louder, louder!

~50 Shades of James~

Dashing round a corner I came face to face with a weathered gypsy calmly strumming his flamenco guitar. "Señor," he said, "un euro, por favor, señor, señor." He strummed a few discordant chords, winking at me from beneath his sombrero. "Boss!" The gypsy hissed, pulling up the hem of his hat. "It is I, James!"

"Unbelievable! What a disguise! And you can play the guitar?"

"No time for that boss. Nice moves. Here – take the medallion and go south, I will delay them as best I can."

*Go away you miserable wretch, you are a scoundrel!

183

James threw over the glittering gold medallion. I opened my trusty rucksack, secreting the medallion in its depths next to the Ark and the Portrait of the Sandals-Grey. It must have taken me no more than ten seconds, but when I glanced back up at James, he was disguised as a priest! Black frock, bible in hand – stood in the centre of the alley, arms akimbo as the capirote horde sounded closer and closer.

"Get a move on Mark!"

Behind me came the sound of a thousand flapping feet, I heard a cry "allí están!"* – I took to my heels running to the far end of the alleyway.

"De rodillas hermanos!"⁺ James called out, raising his bible with one hand and sprinkling holy water from his bottle.

I dived down the nearest narrow street, through an open café, and out the back of a small book store. They had put out an all-stations alert to the 15 cofradías. From the stomp of jack heeled boots and bobbing of pointed hoods I could see them forming a massive perimeter to entrap us within the city limits. Nazarenos of all colours bearing crosses, chains, and candles were gathering. They burnt incense, thick clouds of choking church fragrance filled the streets.

I ran towards la Plaza Mayor desperate for fresh air. Unbeknownst to me las hermandades had just managed to close their encirclement of inner Cácares. They held those weighty sacred effigies aloft on a ritual march, swaying through the thick incense down narrow city streets. At the far side of the plaza I saw an asian tourist. He ran towards the advancing Nazarenos, waving his hands frantically and

*There they are!
+On your knees brothers!

shouting "un foto, un foto! Quere tomar foto, porfi. Amigos, un foto en grupo todos, si, si?"*

In an instant the whole procession thudded to a halt. Every single Nazareno started arguing about their position by seniority of the hermandades, fighting to be foremost. I shook my head in amazement.

Saved at the last by their narcissism, I escaped via three discos, an open air tapas bar and grill, and a quick stop in a hotel bathroom.

Later, I made a second rendezvous with James at a run down four star restaurant on the outskirts of Cáceres.

"You never imagine how lucky I've been." I said, relaying my miraculous escape, all thanks to the asian tourist and the egotism of the Nazarenos.

"Oh?" James smiled, slipping a brown envelop from his bag. "Here, some holiday snapshots you might find interesting."

"Unbelievable!" My shout drew the attention of several off duty Guardia Serrano. The photos were incredible! Each and every one of the hermandades in eccentric poses – the same terrifying parade that had haunted me through the streets! The person behind the lens snapping them could be no other then the tourist himself! James had outwitted us all, myself included!

The Next Day – Back at Devil's Tower Camp, the CO stormed into the 2IC's office. "Do you know anything about this bill I've received for a guitar, a camera and a bible?"

"No," came the curt response. James shook his head and hid a sly smile.

---

*A photo, a photo! I want to take a photo, please. Friends, a group photo, yes, yes?

Hans and his brethren were free. The iron grip of the Nazarenos no more. His people reunited would be at liberty to march home, to keep the Camino safe and open for all.

I strode out early that morning and was witness to a long column of ragged pilgrims, haunched over wooden walking sticks, treading diligently towards the distant Santiago – under the field of stars they strode. I saw Hans, hung about his neck – the medallion. The pilgrims wore ristras de chorizo y morcilla*, a sign perhaps. Maybe they were just hungry.

Hans eyes met mine – with a silent nod we knew and understood the pilgrim's code.

Help those in need.

*Necklaces of chorizo and morcilla.

16

Mission The Seventh

~The Rock and a Hard Place~

Deep within my rucksack slept the Ark. It had been carried for every single step from Cardiff to Gibraltar. This was not something I could have ever accomplished alone – not without the three fearless heroes; Francis – chief strategist, Tammy – communications expert, and James – master of camouflage and concealment.

I knew that many more brave warrior-pilgrims would be assembling at the Red Sands, ready to welcome me home with a bottle of red. This was the Fellowship of the Walk – though I walk alone we are one. Joined in walking, advancing step by step, side by side. My feet cannot move without this vital knowledge – the knowing I walk with everyone who matters to me, who has held me up and kept my feet on the right path. My feet cannot move without the sandals and the sandals come to life on my feet.

There was now a certain special something in the air – the home stretch! The scent of calentita and rosto,* the cry of seagulls, the roar of car horns along la Bateria! I heard it all and was in the highest of high spirits – how could I not be? It was now more than seventy days and two thousand kilometres since I had seen the sands of Eastern Beach, gazed up at the limestone wall of the North Face, or dodged the marauding pack of apes around the Trafalgar Cemetery. I missed my home, missed meeting a hundred friends down

*Two typical Gibraltarian dishes.

Main Street, missed sitting sipping coffee at the Piazza. I had been away for too long – too long! Time to go home.

An open road – the salt taste of the ocean on the breeze, home! Gibraltar! Ahead in clear blue skies a solitary seagull circled. Was I already that close to the coast?

The gull flew closer, crying out and diving down at my head. At the last second it swooped up, dropping a package at my feet. A soggy bundle of papers tied with string – I saw the addressee – TO EL NIÑO BUFANDA. Good God! The Gibraltar Chronicle! Today's edition! Attached to the front was a note;

"Code name Bufanda – read the headlines! – Tammy."

At the top of the page in big bold black type face read "SIEGE LINES REDRAWN AT LA LÍNEA" – A full colour image of the overlord of Iberia, Cyriano Malloy! He stood at the frontier, behind him apartment blocks had been barricaded, the ancient fortifications re-made and coils of barbed wire stretched across the beaches. Beneath the picture; "Iberia Ready Poised To Invade, Gibraltar Isolated From Allies."

I frantically flipped through the pages of the Chronicle. Every article detailed another outrage that had been visited upon Gibraltar – "GIBRALTAR DECLARED DEN OF INEQUITY." Malloy's side-kick, the machiavellian master of propaganda – the Seacock, had been busy spinning a web of deceit and enticing diplomats with gifts of jamón ibérico and the finest chorizos. It was clear that the chairman of the C24 was under the spell of the Ibérico puppet masters. These degenerate miscreants could make millions of euros vanish into the void of abandoned sea side resorts, barren golf courses, and international airports that never received so much as a single plane! They had the power to make people believe that employment is up! That everyone has a job! Only, of course, if they wanted it – incredible! True masters of mass-delusion!

Another headline – "SILOS ARMED, MALLOY PREPARES FOR FINAL COUNTDOWN" – and the article read: Previously thought to only be innocuous grain silos, the Premier of Iberia Cyriano Malloy, has today openly declared that the dozens of recently erected silos in the Medina Sidonia area are, in fact, surface-to-surface missile installations. Our investigations have revealed that there are over fifty rockets primed with deadly payload warheads. Filled to the brim with a noxious mixture of gazpacho, chorizo, churros, topped off generously with chunks of turrón.[*] The foul concoction has been left to ferment into an explosive mixture that Malloy declared was certain to "inevitably make an Iberian out of every last Llanito!"[+]

I threw down the ragged copy of the Chronicle. This could not stand! This aggression could not stand! The silos must be nearby! I'd been walking in the Medina Sidonia area all day and had passed several silo installations. Those hills behind Malloy in the photo, I recognized them – a chalk hill and tall antenna. They were not far from my current position!

Determined, I followed the winding dirt paths away from the Camino and into the polígonos industriales. Spied a multitude of unmarked vans being unloaded of tins of gazpacho and packets of turrón – I had found the spot!

Ahead, up and over the chalk hill and just on the other side, arose a fearful racket of snorts and stomping hooves, of loud oinks and cries of "Malloy! Malloy!" Laying flat and crawling up through the brush I saw the assembly through my trusty pair of binoculars.

*Typical Spanish foods.
+Slang for Gibraltarian.

~Robin Hoods, Robin Hats, Robin Everything~

Cyriano Malloy stood on a podium at the base of a fifty foot gleaming new grain silo. He held up a box with a large red button. Above, the top of the silo opened, the conical red tip of an armed missile slowly rose up out of the cavity, pointing into the blue skies. I counted a dozen silos just in this area, a dozen missiles with armed warheads all aimed at the Rock. Around Malloy were a horde of fat bristle backed porcine, their skin brown and black in patches with fearsome short tusks on either side of scarred snouts. These gristle-backs were the elite of the elite, the core of the legendary Battalion – the Pata Negras, part of the deadly 1st Chorizo Division.

Malloy screamed into his microphone "No more!" He thrust a hand into the air. "Ahora, ya, today! Right now! We will take it back! These missiles, once launched, will fly straight to the very top of the Rock of Gibraltar, their payload will reach every nook and cranny – every single Llanito will inevitably give in to the tastes of La Gran Republica Democratica de Iberia! After today Gibraltar will be no more! Viva Iberia! Viva Malloy!"

An almighty roar went up, the Ibéricos stomped their hooves into the ground, snorting and squealing. I looked on through my binoculars, utterly helpless – too far from the podium to do anything, too late to stop Malloy's finger descending like a thunderbolt from up high and, with a mighty cry of "Ciudadanos – Podemos!"* ringing out over the sound system he thrust his digit down onto the big red button.

...

Nothing.

Silence.

*Citizens – We Can!

Malloy removed his digit. Thrust it again! And again!

Nada.

I looked about, spying movement beyond the silos – there! At the far edge of the militarized farm-compound I saw them; climbing up on the farmhouse roofs and up the electrical poles, stripping the copper and metals and loading them into a rickety truck! Los busca vidas! The non-existent unemployed had nicked all the wire! Malloy slammed his fist into the button again and again, roaring with rage and impotence – the missiles would never launch!

Malloy screamed in frustration, throwing down the button and jumping from the podium. "If the missiles don't work we'll take Gibraltar by force! Vamos muchachos!"* They clambered into waiting white vans and sped off to the south. I followed – on foot, of course, sandals-grey engaged sixth gear, down the dusty tracks like a Seat 500 with Mad Max at the wheel!

My heart weighed heavy, every step drew me inexorably closer to home – I'd not stopped to rest or even have lunch! I used the last of my red wine on the Portrait of Sandals-Grey, it was the only thing that kept me going, kept me upright at all. The power of the portrait kept my feet moving, even as my mind was besieged by the countless visions of horrors that Malloy and his vicious armies were visiting upon Gibraltar my feet never stopped moving.

There, in sight! Gibraltar! The lonely mountain. Surrounded by the Mediterranean Sea, one of the Pillars of Hercules. This was the end of the civilized world, everything beyond this point was unregulated taxi drivers, non Latin derived languages, and strange shop closing times. I could see the levanter forming from its knife-edge ridge.

*Lets go lads!

Walked down, past the refinery and into Campamento. On the outskirts were several squads of armed porcine, outposts had been set up in every café and bar along the road. Taking a leaf out of James' book of disguises, I entered into Lidl, clothing myself in long tube socks, open toed flip-flops, and covering my face with sun cream. Confident that my cover would not be blown, I cracked open a Pilsener and, imbibing from it deeply, set off across the Spanish lines along the beach front.

Ahead was a frontier queue the likes of which I'd never seen. La Línea converted into a massive military camp. The whole sea front had rows and rows of large white tents, an Iberian flag flying above them – a red leg of ham on a field of yellow lard. The fortifications were manned by hundreds of Shock Troops – thousands upon thousands of massive bristle backed cerdos ibéricos – I thought that it must have been the entire Pata Negra battalion now moving up towards the boarder together in a single formation.

I drank deep from my beer, passing by several military units that seemed familiar – the remnants of the Friesian tribe, polishing their horns against grindstones. The last of the All Blacks – scarred, tattered from their thrashing, but determined and full of bile. A cofradía of Nazarenos in full regalia in armoured procession. They were the Penitentes, gold filigree and high blue hoods, the last of the fanatical devotees.

~Sortie Part Deux – Sortie Harder~

Malloy's second-hand man, the inviolable Seacock left in command of the siege. The Seacocks' first action had been to seal off all access to and from the Rock – he ordered that a massive trench the length of the airport, from coast to coast, be dug and filled with tinto de verano. A deadly alcoholic aroma arose from the trench, severely intoxicating any who might approach, creating a no-mans land between La Línea and Gibraltar.

On the far side of the wine filled trench were a number of pitiful individuals sprawled on the ground. They were the brave souls who attempted to cross into Gibraltar only to be entirely inebriated and collapse.

A huge banner stretched the length of the enemy encampment, which I later learnt was made of the remnants of surviving sails from the Great Armada. Embroidered with gold thread from the uniform of 'El Caudillo',* the message on the banner read – "GIBRALTAR – THE PARTY IS OVER".

I needed to get through! I had to cross the wine-filled trench and there was no time to waste – Malloy should be readying to invade at any moment! The true assault would launch as soon as he arrived at the front. From the look of things they would bridge the tinto trench and attack across the airport, directly into the Laguna area. It would be too late to get in by then! I needed to be in Gibraltar before the assault, needed to take the Portrait of Sandals-Grey and the Ark of Cardiff to those besieged – there was only one chance – else all would be lost!

Girded my loins – nothing to it, you see? All this time I'd known I'd walked with a higher purpose – every taberna and bodega, every glass of red wine had fortified my veins, hardened my resolve and prepared me for the tribulation that now I must undergo. I held the Portrait of Sandals-Grey to my chest.

For any normal mortal crossing this trench would inevitably spell their doom. But! My exertions with Francis in the north

*Referring to Franco, meaning diminutive of head.

and James in the south, knew that I could do it! Years of military training had prepared me well for the sacrifice I was about to make; all the mess dinners, all the binge drinking would now pay off! Cross this deadly river of wine, even if I had to drink every last drop!

Dashing between the patrolling guards I threw myself head first into the murky trench!

First my mind went – in an instant I had been thrown into the dizzying world of los borrachos,[*] putting one hand in front of another I swam.

In the thick liquid next to me was another poor fool who'd tried to imbibe his way across in the same fashion. He groaned and grabbed at me, his wine swollen face flushed red. I threw him off, struggled forward holding my rucksack over my head.

Gasping for air I pulled myself up on the far side, sliding out of the muddy earth and falling into a puddle of wine. I could not move, the world spun like a thousand carnival rides. I spluttered and lay still, letting the Portrait of Sandals-Grey fall to my side.

~Behold a Miracle~

A miracle! A light shone from the Portrait of Sandals-Grey, a truly divine light! Within my head resounded a single thought – a single deed that I must do right – put the sandals on! Wear them!

I did – fumbling and slipping my own worn sandals off, I reached into the glowing light of the painting. The Portrait shimmered with an unearthly radiance, I plucked from the drawn lines and masterful brush strokes the pair of holy

*Drunkards.

relics and placed them on the ground. Affixing the straps with the greatest of reverence to my feet, in an instant my mind became clear – the fog of inebriation vanished.

I crossed over to Gibraltar at last, through the ruins of the airport and the torn up barriers that had once been the customs offices. Forward, passing under the barrier and onto the cracked tarmac and ruinous runway.

I was through, standing on sacred British ground. The siege collapsed, 1st Chorizo Division withdrew, the dust settled and peace came with it. It was the Ark. It had reached its destination and had fulfilled its destiny, it had made everything right...

It was all over – everything, I had done it! My quest was at an end!

But...

~Aporkalypse Now~

From the Ibérico siege lines along the whole of La Línea came a rumble and a mechanical roar. An inhuman howl of rage erupted from a thousand throats, the air filled with a grind and furious squeal of tires – there! Comandante Cyriano Malloy up on a podium on the back of a truck. Squatting beside him in a black leather gimp outfit, a tall vile man; side kick – the Seacock!

The combined Iberian Army, a swell of thousands surging towards my position, laying long planks to cross the tinto trench, swarming through the ruins and rubble. I ran – picking up my rucksack, the exhaustion and feeling of the thousands of kilometres giving way to a new found energy surging up my legs, entering into my bones. The Sandals! They were lending their strength to me in this, my hour of need!

Ran to la Laguna and – BANG! BOOM! A massive cannonade from the upper galleries on the North Face. A wall of metal and shrapnel tore into the Iberian front ranks reducing the foremost troops to shredded pork.

Past Victoria Stadium, up Winston Churchill Avenue. I heard a rally cry – "Get them lads!" Sortieing out (down from Sortie Road) were G, I and B Companies, taking up defensive positions at the roundabout. Following them in full regalia marched the Regimental Band flying the colours – thumping out on battle worn drums and gleaming bagpipes the glorious 'Cock of the North'. The Iberian Army had reformed their ranks, the elite Pata Negras to the fore, fearsome brave beasts that they were, charging at us through the cannonade.

Here we were – the thin red and grey line, assembled against the might of the whole beastly Iberian horde.

We stood alone. I picked up a fallen rifle of someone struck down by an All Black hatchet, taking a position within the roundabout. We were forced to make a fighting retreat, back up Winston Churchill Avenue, releasing volley after volley of fire into the indomitable foe. Thought it was over – the Portrait of Sandals-Grey had got me this far. The Ark! Maybe the answer lay in the Ark of Cardiff! I struggled with my rucksack, but! At that moment two giant ham beasts broke through the line, using a butchers bill-hook they swiped my trusty rucksack from my hands. All was lost!

I'm not proud of this you know – I turned and I fled. Ran, like a coward! I legged it to Grand Casemates Square, falling exhausted on a heap of cigarette cartons. Was this it? Were we to fall here? Retreating behind our walls and waiting for our doom? It would be nigh on impossible to weather such a storm, to hold out alone against this furious assault.

The horde charged. A riot of roars and ear shattering battle cries. Malloy rode in their midst, high on his chariot podium. This was the end, the end my friend, the bitter end.

But... What's that?

Hark, in the distance yonder!

I saw – behind the advancing Ibérico armies approached a multitude – many times greater than the besieging foe -

There!

~The Passion of the Crisps~

From beyond the siege lines of La Línea, from every back road, and from the forest and mountain paths. There! Clad in gleaming white vests and adorned with sashes of red frippery they came, riding polished wooden carriages tied to polished horses dressed in bells. They came, gitano guitarists playing flamenco, cries of Olé!

In our most desperate straits – at the end of our rope, la Romería* had come! The people of Iberia out to do the one thing they did the very best – have a fiesta! Forks and knives and paper plates at the ready, war cries like "quien tiene la torta patata?"+ and "vamos a la playa jajajaja".±

Taken from the rear by such a vastly superior force, the Ibérico armies collapsed – no more than a paper tiger when confronted with true might. The strength of a people united in celebration. Cyriano Malloy and his vile sidekick, the Seacock, vanished the very moment it seemed that their battle plans went awry.

*A religious celebration consisting of a trip on floats and horses and a picnic in the countryside.
+Who has the torta patata?
±Lets go to the beach, jajajaja.

Victory. Gibraltar was safe once more! But, we were not rescued by distant allies, no. We had been saved at the last by our closest friends, the people most like us with whom we share more than a common bond or common history. United by a higher ideal – a singular purpose that transcends all the small miserly differences. Our neighbours from el Campo de Gibraltar had come in our hour of need.

Hands reached down to pick me up – Francis and James, tattered and worn from the fighting.

"Well done Mark". Francis slapped me heartily on my back.

"Good to see you, boss." James said.

Then I heard another voice, "welcome home dad". Tammy hugged me, handing over my battle weary rucksack.

I was home. After all this time, after all this wine, after all – home, safe and sound. My mind wandered – how had I ended up here? This strange world! From Cardiff I'd carried the Ark the length of Iberia. I'd borne witness to all manner of bizarre creatures, of half human beasts – of animals wielding morcilla – was this all a dream? Had I fallen into a coma? A wine induced stupor? Some nightmare state that I simply could not wake from?

"!" I exclaimed.

"You alright boss?" James said.

"I've got it! The Druid! It all started with that bloody Druid in Cheddar Gorge!"

"What did, boss?" James gave me a queer eye, but that was normal for him.

"The Druid gave me that hippy cheese! It must have been drugged! Blast his eyes! That bloody Druid and his bloody wicker hat and weird cheeses!"

"You want some more, boss?" James said with a wicked grin. In a flash he pulled out a mighty long scraggly beard and affixed it to his ears, placing a wicker cap about his head. "It was just plain Cheddar from the QM's ration box, boss. A little out of date maybe, but you know cheese, that stuff never goes off."

"You? You were the Druid all along?"

"Sure boss, why not?" James chuckled.

~All That for This?~

Later that same day in the ruins of Casemates we all stood together – Tammy, Francis, James, the CO, all the survivors of the Fifteenth Siege of Gibraltar. This was the moment. I'd only carried the spark, brought with me the flame from distant lands. The fire, the passion of every Llanito would never die. I opened the wooden casket of the Ark, retrieving and reading at last the words I'd carried from Cardiff to Gibraltar;

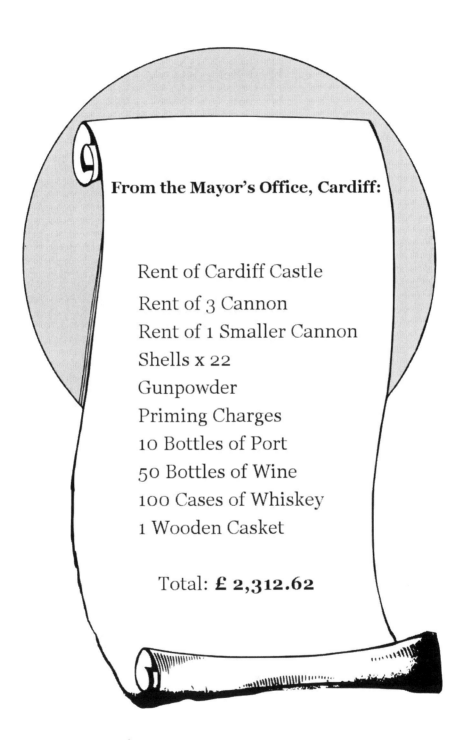

From the Mayor's Office, Cardiff:

Rent of Cardiff Castle

Rent of 3 Cannon

Rent of 1 Smaller Cannon

Shells x 22

Gunpowder

Priming Charges

10 Bottles of Port

50 Bottles of Wine

100 Cases of Whiskey

1 Wooden Casket

Total: **£ 2,312.62**

17

That Café in Gibraltar

Mark: "And that's the whole thing, more or less. Well, more or less." He sipped his café con leche, contemplating the coffee bill.

Matt: "You done? You sure? No more rubbish left to speak?" I said, sipping coffee in a similar fashion, not even looking at the bill.

Mark: "I'm done. Promise. That's it, the whole tale – from top to bottom, start to finish – that's everything as it really happened. Cross my heart and hope to die." He said, as he crossed his chest.

Matt: "I don't believe it. I've heard it all dad, and there ain't a word of truth to it."

Mark: "C'mon Matt, would I lie to you?"

Matt: "Yes. Very much so yes," I said. "The Druid was James? That doesn't even make sense – was he even in England at the time? And the animals – I mean, I understand you were going for a metaphor or something, but having the people of Iberia be pigs and cows? Isn't that a bit too much?"

Mark: "Come on, don't be like that. They weren't all half-animals, only some. I told you its just reality, part of the truth, you can't escape that!" He sat still for a moment. "I know! Right, take a look at this! Look! Look and see that every word I spoke was The Truth! Look!"

He held the mirror up to my face and there I saw reflected a snout and small blue piggy eyes – I was one of them!

I was one of them all along!

Matt: "Wait. That doesn't make sense."

Mark: "Who is paying the bill, you?"

Matt: "It makes perfect sense Dad," I quickly got to my trottered feet. "I never doubted you for a second."

Mark: "Good lad, now write it all down, exactly like I've told it to you."

And I did.

Kit List

Item	Weight (g)
Rucksack (Golite Jam 50 l)	880
Walking poles	560
Water proof stuff sacks x 2	150
Water bottle (1 Litre collapsible)	50
Inov-8 shoes	750
Source Gobi Sandals	700
Soft shoes	100
Shoe carrying case x 2	100
Maps/cases/guidebooks/etc	400
Tablet & ancillaries	350
Tel & ancillaries	200
Torches/battery	100
Massage tools	150
Wash & hygiene	300
Medical pack	400
Knee & ankle supports	350
Glasses x 2 + case	100
Hat	50
Neck scarf/Buff	50
Socks x 2 pairs	50
Underpants (Lowe Alpine)	80
Gloves x 2 pairs	100
Woolly hat (North Face)	75
Marmot Precip Jkt	350

Rab Microlight(down)Jkt...380

Rab Nimbus Windtop Jkt..125

Rab Cirrus Pull-on...75

Long sleeve shirt...150

North Face t-shirt...125

Berghaus waterproof trousers..250

North Face convertible trousers...200

Shorts...125

Wallet & contents...250

Watch..50

Neck cord/dog tag/lucky charm..50

Food..600

Water..2000-5000

Total..8775 + water

Facts and Figures

Days walked – 68

Rest days – 7

Start – 21st Apr 2015, Cardiff Castle

End – 04th Jul 2015, Casemates, Gibraltar

Total distance – 2201 km

Average distance walked – 32.7 km/day

Number of steps – 4.44 million

Worst day – day 23

Best day – day 75

Highlights – Cardiff, Santiago, meeting my walking companions

Essential kit – Source Sandals

Most used item – underpants (now in retirement drawer next to the 'pants of Randall' – running shorts used for four years! Ex G Coy lads will understand)

Least used item – waterproof gloves

Number of Hats lost – 2

Number of times I got lost – none. Really. Zero, I don't get lost

Number of Cities I did not get lost in – 13

Water consumed – 3 to 5 litres a day

Vitamins/energy tablets taken – none

Haircut – one in Astorga, beard trim too

Tubs of Tiger Balm – 3

Tubs of Vaseline – 4

Tubs of Vicks VapoRub – 7

Bottles of red wine consumed – 53 ¾

Showers taken – far too many!

Lessons Learnt

- I am happier with the wind in my face and the sun on my head.
- Stick to sandals.
- Avoid unnecessary baggage.
- Plan rest days and spread them out.
- Have confidence in your ability but understand your limitations.
- Spend time talking to people and assimilating your surroundings.
- Be flexible to changing circumstances.
- Take one day at the time, step by step, little by little.
- Learn how to recognise the good around you.
- Make the most of the moment.
- Follow your true path.

A Dream of the Future...

It began on the black waters at the bottom of the well, a speck on the reflection of the moon. Pin prick of light that seemed to crawl between the constellations, gathering inexorable momentum and drawing the other reflected dots of light in it's wake. Slowly, surely, an invisible net catching every star, pulling them all to the east.

I watched the waters of the well. If I dared raise my head, if I looked up would the stars be there? It may be just a ripple in the well waters, nothing more. If I looked would the moon be a black circle against a black sky?

So, every time I would wait, the dream the same. Stare and wait for the waters to calm. At last, at last, wait and stare, the waters would not calm. The stars had gone, every single speck of light gone gone gone.

Waited for night to become day, it was not to be. Sun would not come, waters still and moon dark. A moment of perfection, perfect calm, perfect stillness, perfect dream that slow perfect black becomes.

All the stars all the lights followed that speck, and so must I. Go, follow the stars, follow the light. I must go, must follow the stars –

I dream of walking to the east...

***

Matt: "I know! A sequel! Yeah!"

Mark: "What shall we call it?"

211

Matt: "I dunno, uh, what about Walk from the Rock? You know, cause you're starting from here?"

Mark: "Don't be stupid. Think, come on Matt, you're good with coming up with stuff like that."

Matt: "Ok, ok. What about this, Walk to Jerusalem? That fits, no?"

Mark: "Nah, we've already done one walk to thingy, gotta do something else."

Matt: "How about doing a cook book instead of a diary? I mean, neither of us really know how to cook, but, well..."

Mark: "That's perfect!"

Matt: "Really?"

Mark: "Yeah! That's great! We'll walk from Gibraltar up to Santiago, then on to Rome, and from Rome to Jerusalem – all the while we'll collate recipes from the various Caminos and regions and put them together in a cook book. It'll be great! Yeah!"

Matt: "Wait, wait, wait – you want me to walk with you?"

Mark: "Yes! I mean, why wouldn't you want to? Its great, no? Come on, come walking, you'll love it. All the people and places and bottles of wine, come on Matt, it'll be fantastic!"

Matt: "..."

Mark: "Matt? Matthew? Where'd you go? "

Matt: "..."

MARK RANDALL is a retired Lieutenant Colonel with 26 years military service. An avid long distance hiker with a dozen Caminos under his belt. Has a Masters in International Liaison and Communication and was awarded the Gibraltar Medal of Distinction for services to his Regiment. When not walking he can be found exploring mountain areas in his ageing campervan, cooking and blowing his bellowing bagpipes. Once managed to get lost three times in an Ikea in a single visit.

MATTHEW RANDALL has a passion for reading, writing, cooking (not to his dad's taste), and cigars. Born and bred in Gibraltar but schooled for a long time in Germany and the UK. Collects fountain pens, empty jars, typewriters, and peculiar words and phrases. He spends far too much time navigating while in the caravan and has avoided getting lost throughout Spain, Portugal and France.

Printed in Great Britain
by Amazon